SCN EDITIONS

General Editors: J. Max Patr

Volume

THE INWARD TEACHER

Milton's Rhetoric of Christian Liberty

By

James Egan

The University of Akron

University Park, Pennsylvania
Seventeenth-Century News
The Pennsylvania State University
1980

The Inward Teacher:

Milton's Rhetoric of Christian Liberty

By

James Egan

The University of Akron

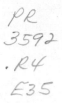
FOR KATHY AND MOLLY

CONTENTS

Acknowledgements

I have received valuable assistance of many kinds in preparing this monograph. A Grant-in-Aid of Research from The Newberry Library enabled me to complete my preliminary investigations. Three Faculty Research Grants from The University of Akron financed additional study. The University and the Department of English provided me with vitally necessary released time to write several drafts. To the following University officials I am especially indebted: Claibourne E. Griffin, Dean of Graduate Studies and Research; Noel L. Leathers, Vice President and Provost; and Robert A. Oetjen, Dean of Buchtel College of Arts and Sciences. Without their generous financial support this work could not have been published. I have benefitted in ways too numerous to mention from the scholarly expertise of Professors J. Max Patrick and Harrison T. Meserole, editors of *Seventeenth-Century News*. As he has done so often, Lowell Coolidge, Professor Emeritus, The College of Wooster, again offered his advice and encouragement. Robert and Helen Petrusic and the Holy Ghost Fathers of Ewing Avenue helped in ways they will easily recognize. Finally, the manuscript might never have been completed unless the love, patience, and inspiration of my wife, Kathleen, had been with me.

Chapter Five, originally entitled "Public Truth and Personal Witness in Milton's Last Tracts," has already been published, in a somewhat different form, in *ELH, A Journal of English Literary History*, 40 (Summer 1973), 231-48. I am grateful to The Johns Hopkins University Press for permission to reprint.

The Augustinian Imperative

Christian liberty, Milton claimed in the *Second Defence*, was the primary ideal which prompted him to enter the struggle to perfect Reformation and which sustained him in his polemic labors: "true and substantial liberty, which must be sought, not without, but within, and which is best achieved not by the sword, but by a life rightly conducted. . . . there are, in all, three varieties of liberty without which civilized life is scarcely possible, namely ecclesiastical liberty, domestic or personal liberty, and civil liberty."[1] The fact that a clear majority of Milton's pamphlets may be interpreted as pleas for the "varieties of liberty" enumerated above lays to rest any doubts about his determination to advance the cause he cherished. For several reasons, however, these memorable lines cannot stand as a definition of Milton's views on Christian liberty. As Arthur Barker points out, Milton did not conceptualize his theory of liberty as early as his remarks in the *Second Defence* intimate, and the theory underwent substantive change during the prose period.[2] Moreover, neither the passage itself nor its immediate context in the tract offers an explicitly Christian view of liberty. Milton's most exacting statement on the subject, one which holds true for his entire pamphleteering career, occurs in the *Christian Doctrine*:

> CHRISTIAN LIBERTY means that CHRIST OUR LIBERATOR FREES US FROM THE SLAVERY OF SIN AND THUS FROM THE RULE OF THE LAW AND OF MEN, AS IF WE WERE EMANCIPATED SLAVES. HE DOES THIS SO THAT, BEING MADE SONS INSTEAD OF SERVANTS AND GROWN MEN INSTEAD OF BOYS, WE MAY SERVE GOD IN CHARITY THROUGH THE GUIDANCE OF THE SPIRIT OF TRUTH. (VI, 537)

Milton's complete discussion of these postulates in the *Christian Doctrine* isolates most of his major premises about liberty and implies others. The Pauline context of Milton's assumptions is familiar enough. Like most of his Protestant contemporaries, he equated the essence of Christian freedom with the dispensation from the shackles of the Mosaic Law attained through Christ's Covenant of Redemption. Above all, Christian freedom, the inheritance of true believers, was synonymous for Milton with an inward state. The bearers of Christian liberty were "not the recipients of a peculiar spiritual experience,"[3] for their freedom rested upon ethical foundations and was, therefore, communicable and transferable, not solipsistic. Properly nourished, that freedom would grow until it embraced and transformed church and state. Although he stressed the ethical nature of freedom, Milton accepted the traditional qualification that virtuous actions could not in themselves, without the redemptive sacrifice of Christ, merit salvation.

If, as Northrop Frye maintains, Milton conceived of liberty as the "condition in which genuine action is possible,"[4] it necessarily follows that the possessor of it must guard his inner freedom. Only if he succeeds in keeping secular concerns properly subordinated to the needs of the spirit and in seeking out and combating his enemies in the unregenerate world will he be entitled to the moral privileges conferred upon him by liberty. Perhaps the foremost privilege is the gift of prophecy. The regenerate are known by the high degree of spiritual sensitivity apparent in their words and deeds, and committed to expressing verbally the life-giving truths they have witnessed. Christian liberty also imparts considerable authority in the secular sphere. Throughout the prose period Milton defended the right of regenerate Christians to offer political guidance to the people and to their leaders. Milton's own tracts support his contention that the regenerate are likewise obligated to present reasonable justifications of their positions so that others would adopt them. Only in the extreme circumstances of 1659-1660 did Milton follow to its inevitable conclusion the principle that regenerate men hold unique political privileges. His advocacy of a perpetual senate in *The Readie Way* implies a belief, however reluctant, that in order to prevent further backsliding into godlessness, regenerate leaders must govern, even if they offer little reasonable justification for their exercise of power. Such an alternative, he was forced to conclude, was preferable to rule by the unregenerate who had given themselves in bondage to their own vices. Milton's decision to fight God's battle for Reformation was a measure of his conviction that universal spiritual concord, the realization of the New Jerusalem on earth, would follow inevitably and in the foreseeable future upon the apprehension and practice of Christian freedom.

His varied arguments for liberty of conscience, church, and state disclose a thorough indebtedness to the Christian rhetorical tradition which flowed down from Augustine through Luther and Calvin. Augustine's rhetorical precepts are synthetic. In molding classical rhetorical formulae to Christian homiletics, Augustine did not deny eloquence to the Christian orator, nor did he forbid a knowledge of classical rhetorical theory;[5] he merely cautioned that oratorical eloquence must not be an end in itself. One might expect the Christian rhetorician, therefore, to be familiar with the principle of decorum stated by Cicero in *Orator*: "the same style and the same thoughts must not be used in portraying every condition in life, or every rank, position or age, and in fact a similar distinction must be made in respect of place, time, and audience. The universal rule, in oratory as in life, is to consider propriety. This depends on the subject under discussion, and on the character of both the speaker and the audience."[6] He would be conversant with the conventional, ultimately Aristotelian, tripartite division of oratory into the deliberative (which urged men to expedient action or dissuaded them from what was harmful), the forensic (used to defend the just and to attack the unjust), and the epideictic (used for praising and blaming);[7] with the five-part structure of an oration, namely exordium, narration, partition, confirmation and refutation, peroration; with the argumentative strategies enumerated in Cicero's *Topica*; and with the categories of proof furnished by Aristotle in the *Rhetoric*: "The first kind depends on the personal character of the speaker; the second on putting the audience into a certain frame of mind; the third on the proof, or apparent proof, provided by the words of the speech itself."[8] Aristotle's "modes of persuasion" are, of course, familiar to rhetoricians as ethical, pathetic, and logical proof.

The Christian orator would, moreover, be aware of the distinct personalities and functions of classical oratorical style. Cicero diagrams the high style as follows: "The style is brilliant if the words employed are chosen for their dignity and used metaphorically and in exaggeration . . . and in harmony with the actual action and the representation of the facts."[9] Abundant, expert use of metaphor and simile lends grandeur to the style, while schemes of sound and word order and rhythmic devices lend grace and ornateness. Quintilian's demand that the orator "exalt his style by amplification and rise even to *hyperbole*"[10] singles out the fictive devices, apostrophe and *prosopopoeia*, native to it; the transformation of literal and factual into metaphoric and hyperbolic induces the elaborate emotional reaction desired by the orator. Finally, the tone of the high style must convey a sustained intensity so as to move the audience effectively. Both Cicero and Quintilian agreed that the peroration was the most appropriate place for the high style, although it could be employed in a digression and, on occasion, in the exordium. In *Orator*, Cicero scrutinizes the low style:

> [One] must avoid all the figures that I have described above, such as clauses of equal length, with similar endings or identical cadences, and the studied charm produced by the change of a letter, lest the elaborate symmetry and a certain grasping after a pleasant effect be too obvious. . . . Other figures of speech [the orator] will be able to use freely, provided only he breaks up and divides the periodic structure and uses the commonest of words and the mildest of metaphors.[11]

In the low style we should not expect to encounter the alluring metaphors, "rich, diversified and copious diction," and rhythmic devices of the high style. Since its primary purpose is to advance logical proof and state facts with acumen, it predominates in the confirmation and refutation of an oration. However, in the *Ad Herennium* the urbane, conversational quality of the style is stressed, suggesting a duty separate from that of logical argument; as an example of the plain style at work the author of the *Ad Herennium* mentions the narration of an oration.[12] The low style, then, may relate facts and reactions in the direct, unadorned manner of refined conversation. When Cicero allows "humour and wit" to the orator who chooses the low style, he points to yet another of the style's functions: satire.[13] Low diction and various species of wit might appear in a passage of straightforward logical argument as a means of marshalling pathetic proof in the form of ridicule.

Cicero approaches the middle style in this manner: "there is perhaps a minimum of vigour, and a maximum of charm. For it is richer than the unadorned style, but plainer than the ornate and opulent style. . . . . To the same oratorical style . . . belong all figures of language, and many of thought."[14] Evidently, the middle style cannot be categorized precisely, for its attributes are realized largely in contrast to those of the high and low styles. While the middle style has recourse to metaphor and to all the "figures of language, and many of thought," it lacks the sustained tonal intensity and metaphoric cast of the high style. The middle style might be valuable in presenting an argument in a heightened tone and with more allusiveness and figurative language than would be permitted in the low style, or as a means of transition between passages in the other two styles.

Milton's mastery of oratorical technique in the *Prolusions* and the *Defences*, respectively, has been explicated by Joseph Anthony Wittreich, Jr., in " 'The Crown of Eloquence': The Figure of the Orator in Milton's Prose Works," in *Achievements of the Left*

Hand: Essays on the Prose of John Milton, ed. Michael Lieb and John Shawcross (Amherst: Univ. of Massachusetts Press, 1974), pp. 28-42; and by A. Robin Bowers in "Milton and Salmasius: The Rhetorical Imperatives," *PQ,* 52 (1973), 55-68, and in "John Milton as Controversialist: Rhetorical Influences on the Structure of the Three *Defences,*" Diss. Princeton 1968. I shall demonstrate that mastery in his English tracts. Of greater significance than Milton's facility with particular oratorical ploys is his profound awareness of the demands of rhetorical decorum. Milton's couching his arguments for liberty in discrete rhetorical genres reveals how well he understood the sophisticated strategies needed to move different audiences. Because the oration afforded a wide range of stylistic and structural tactics, it was the genre he preferred and used for the most public writing of his polemic career. *Areopagitica* and *The Tenure of Kings and Magistrates,* representative orations, are inaugural, composed not in response to an opponent's jibes, but in response to the Christian orator's mandate to speak out on issues of importance for Reformation. In these works Milton spoke to a vast audience consisting not only of his countrymen, but of all who professed interest in Reformation. His audience was again broad in the *History of Britain,* and in it he aspired to assess the deeds of a people who had been favored of God in the seventeenth century as well as in the distant past. To record the behavior of God's Englishmen would be to underline their recurrent failure to act in harmony with Providence. Such a document, if published in mid-Revolution, could have alerted the nation to the need to maintain the elect moral character required of those who would hope to reform Reformation. Milton's decision to withhold the *History* until 1670 implies a substantive change in the motives which prompted him to write it.

Milton did, certainly, have occasion to answer the charges of specific opponents. Utilizing the conventional methodology of point-by-point refutation, he rose to meet the challenges of scholarly authors in *Prelatical Episcopacy* and *Tetrachordon.* The intricate logical exposition, qualification and rebuttal, and exacting citation of sources which permeate these tracts link them with the Renaissance art of disputation. In his last major political pamphlets, those of 1659-1660, Milton communicated effectively with an even narrower audience. Hoping to define for all who would hear him the multifold implications of Christian liberty, Milton wrote plainly and clearly in the style literary historians have customarily connected with the Age of Dryden. Designed to present his case in the most direct, succinct manner possible, Milton's rhetoric is modeled upon a species of discourse destined to evolve into the Restoration sermon. Yet the polemical thrusts of the last tracts are persuasive evidence of Milton's growing recognition that his pleas for liberty were likely to fall on deaf ears.

The narrative presence which dominates the prose reveals yet another Miltonic debt to the Christian homiletic tradition. Milton is more than an orator, for he assumes prophetic responsibilities as a consequence of his Christian freedom. *The Reason of Church-Government* contains the most emphatic declaration of Milton's prophetic license:

> For surely to every good and peaceable man it must in nature needs be a hatefull thing to be the displeaser, and molester of thousands; much better would it like him doubtlesse to be the messenger of gladnes and contentment, which is his chief intended busines, to all mankind, but that they resist and oppose their own true happinesse. But when God commands to take the trumpet and blow a dolorous or a jarring blast, it lies not in mans will what he shall say, or what he shall conceal.   (I, 803)

Milton's prophetic stature carries with it a moral obligation and a spiritual insight which transcend the merely nationalistic concerns of the orator.[15] Although prophecy is the right of all who attain Christian freedom, Milton considered the public character and scope of his mandate extraordinary even among the regenerate. The familiar autobiographical digressions scattered throughout the prose vindicate his worthiness to proclaim the Lord's message. Collectively, the digressions delineate Milton as a man who is uncommonly dedicated to the cause of Reformation, whose life is free from moral corruption, and who accepts the role of prophet even though he knows full well that scorn and vilification will often be his lot. For one so uniquely qualified, a refusal to "speak to the nations" would have been tantamount to defying Providence. Milton's prophetic responsibilities are twofold: celebration and denunciation. The message of "gladnes and contentment" that he would prefer to deliver would be a utopian prefiguration of Reformation perfected evoked in the imagination as, for example, in *Areopagitica*. In the main, however, Milton must direct a "dolorous or a jarring blast" at those institutions or individuals who would impede Reformation. As Milton insists in the *Christian Doctrine*, the Lord's spokesman need not mince words with the recalcitrant: "No consideration is to be shown, however, to the malicious or the obstinate" (VI, 540). In defense of the harsh rhetoric of excoriation occasionally necessary for the prophet, Milton cites the Christian rhetorical tradition: to the Remonstrant's charge that the *Animadversions* was "a slanderous and scurrilous libel," Milton replied that if the accusation referred to his speaking freely concerning "things amisse in religion, but establisht by act of State," then he failed to see "how *Wickleffe* and *Luther*, with all the first Martyrs, and reformers, could avoid the imputation of libelling" also (*An Apol.*, I, 878). For Luther, Wyclif, and Milton, satiric denunciation was a religious tool efficacious in bringing to light the antagonists of Reformation. If Christ himself did not refrain from vehement language (*Animad.*, I, 663), then his prophets need not fear the rebuke that their harshness violates Christian charity.

A far-reaching and little noted influence of Christian homiletic upon Milton's prose appears in the aesthetic progression that unifies and transforms the different genres he uses when he argues for liberty. Despite their obvious differences, these genres are rendered congruent by a common rhetorical evolution from logical to affective arguments, from literal and factual frames of reference to imaginative ones, from contemplative detachment to polemic engagement. This Miltonic tendency grows out of the Augustinian emphasis, particularly in the *Confessions*,[16] on the spiritual faculty of memory, an emphasis perhaps born of Augustine's distrust of fallen human reason. Distinct from the rational and analytical faculties, memory is the fountainhead of spiritual powers, equally capable of recollecting the past and of anticipating the future. Another primary Augustinian influence on the Miltonic aesthetic is the thesis of Augustine's *Christian Doctrine*, Book IV, in its entirety. There Augustine insists that orator and audience progress from outer realities to inner ones, from literal to symbolic, from words to vision.[17] In Platonic fashion, then, Augustine postulates an epistemology which places eternal and immutable knowledge at the end of a vexing ascent through the realms of the temporal and the mutable.[18] Rather than accepting Plato's premise that the Ideas we ultimately seek were transmitted to us in a previous existence, Augustine made God himself responsible for implanting the Ideas in the human mind.[19] For Milton as for Augustine, the highest truths are moral in nature, perpetual reflections of the Divine Mind.

Milton's rhetoric bears out his conviction, shared with Augustine, that a purely rational approach to Christian truth is incomplete and unsatisfying, for to know God rationally is to know him merely in the mind, not in the heart. Only when one engages fully his powers of thinking, feeling, and willing does he become recep-

tive to truth.[20] In all of the genres examined below, Milton's
climactic rhetorical appeals are made to fundamental Christian
beliefs and to memory and imagination but not to reason.[21] These
appeals draw upon the reader's faith in the integrity of Scripture
and in God's Covenant of Reformation, upon the good will of regenerate men, and upon apocalyptic yearning to see Reformation
achieved. If Christian rhetoric is to make the hearer responsive to
the "inward Teacher,"[22] it must penetrate the rational and factual
exterior of events to their spiritual essence. Milton accomplishes
this breakthrough with the aid of the rhetorical catalysts of *pathos*
and *ethos*. As did his Anglican contemporary, John Donne, Milton
sought the conviction of the heart through the medium of figurative language.[23] Milton's climactic pleas inevitably attempt to
make the reader receptive to spiritual truths by bringing those
truths dramatically to life in the imagination.

Not only do Milton's pathetic appeals escalate in intensity and
sophistication as his arguments rise to a crescendo, but his narrative presence becomes increasingly evident as well. The narrator
manifests his profound spiritual insight in the form of forceful
assertions of faith and moral sensitivity. These moral assertions,
which often assume a polemic cast, are simultaneously expressions
of the persona's divinely inspired moral authority, and of his regenerate spiritual temperament as Milton defined it in the *Christian Doctrine*. Milton characterizes the regenerate man as one who,
having been reborn in the New Law, is gifted with a heightened
"understanding of spiritual affairs" (VI, 478), and set apart by the
depth of his faith (VI, 471). The regenerate man commits himself
to a lifelong struggle for moral perfection (VI, 482). In short, the
voice of Milton the pamphleteer, marked by an apocalyptic perspective and language uniquely his own, rises in pitch in successive
arguments within a tract and in successive tracts within a genre,
frequently culminating in a prophetic statement, the ultimate assertion of moral authority. Milton's prophecies remind us that his
is an exemplary voice, an idealized version of Christian integrity
and courage, an instrument for announcing the wishes of Providence. Joan Webber has observed an analogue to the "public-to-
personal" paradigm discussed above in her study of the antipre-
latical tracts. She notes that as Milton proceeds from pamphlet to
pamphlet his rhetoric grows more "personal" and less "public" and
utilitarian, until in the last treatise, *An Apology*, Milton speaks "at
least as much for himself as for his hearers."[24] As I shall later
argue, the development from "public" to "personal" stances typ-
ifies the rhetoric of the entire prose period.

The cumulative effect of his pathetic and ethical pleading is regenerative. In addition to making the reader receptive to the conviction of the heart, Milton exemplifies in his rhetorical persona the regenerate reaction to those spiritual truths he wishes to evoke in the reader. The poet becomes true poem. One is led by Milton's rhetoric to examine his relationship to the Scripturally ordained principles of the Christian religion, particularly to freedom. Grasped by faith, such principles are made operative through an act of the will, so that the reader may set out to explore the "paradise within." The movement of Milton's rhetoric from "the book to the internal scripture,"[25] then, parallels "the Augustinian movement of the mind toward God, drawn by intuitive knowledge of the happiness that lies beyond the bounds of man."[26]

My primary intention in this study will be to demonstrate that Milton presented his arguments for liberty in discrete prose genres selected according to his conception of the audience for whom he wrote. In order to verify that Milton worked with familiar Renaissance genres, it will be necessary to review briefly the rhetorical conventions of the oration, the disputation, the history, and the sermon. After the conventions have been reviewed, the uses to which Milton put them will be examined in detail. Utilizing traditional rhetorical terminology, I will stress dialectical and structural patterns, figurative language, syntax, and authorial persona.[27] Milton's modifications of these genres will be explored as well. When the extent and purpose of Milton's modifications are known, it becomes evident that he was not a mere imitator, but a skilled rhetorician aware of the changing demands of his audience and capable of adapting his rhetoric to satisfy those demands. The length of this study does not permit a discussion of Milton's mixed rhetorical modes, those which cross the boundaries of genre. One noteworthy instance is the second edition (1644) of the *Doctrine and Discipline of Divorce* whose structure is oratorical yet whose method of argument is primarily disputative. Nor have I touched on Milton's style of satirical rebuttal prominent in the *Animadversions* and *Colasterion*, having done so elsewhere.[28] My analyses of Milton's disputations and the sermons of 1659-1660 are comprehensive, covering all tracts written in those genres. Otherwise, as in the case of the orations and histories, I have selected representative examples. As noted earlier, I will likewise examine the progression from factual to evocative perspectives which marks each of Milton's major genres. Variations in this paradigm do, of course, occur, and attention will be given to the nature of such variations.

My secondary purpose in this study will be to point out two significant transformations, one thematic and the other stylistic, during the prose period. The first involves Milton's conception of Christian liberty and of the audience for whom he wrote. In the main, the pamphlets of the 1640's reflect a harmonious Miltonic vision of liberty and of the possibilities for attaining it, while conceptual and rhetorical disjunctives dominate the tracts of the 1650's. Milton gradually came to appreciate the difficulties of trying to reform an intractable nation. I will also argue that over the course of his pamphleteering career, Milton's rhetoric evolves from ornateness and complexity into plainness and simplicity in terms of dialectical and structural tendencies, the employment of tropes and schemes, and the function of authorial persona.

I anticipate that a rhetorical analysis such as mine will contribute to our knowledge of Milton in several ways. Milton's academic training in rhetoric has been discussed thoroughly, notably by Harris Fletcher and D. L. Clark,[29] yet connections have rarely been drawn between Milton's training and his actual practices as a pamphleteer. Moreover, with few exceptions,[30] earlier stylistic studies of the prose have confined themselves to a limited number of pamphlets, a limited period of time, or both, and thereby created a somewhat misleading impression of the variety and sophistication of Milton's rhetoric. An historical, generic approach ought to offset such critical tendencies to particularize by establishing a context broad enough to reveal major trends operative during the prose period. Secondly, a rhetorical explication of Milton's prose will deepen our understanding of the role of rhetoric in his poetry. That much Miltonic verse draws upon the conventions of rhetoric is well known — for example, the debates between the Lady and Comus, Satan's oratory in *Paradise Lost* and Dalila's in *Samson Agonistes*, and the varying styles of *Paradise Lost*. Although I will not deal with the poetry itself, my work should lead to a greater awareness of some of the numerous correlations between Milton's prose and verse rhetoric, and, perhaps, provide some bases for future studies of the rhetorical principles fundamental to both the prose and the verse. Finally, to learn of Milton's mastery of prose genres, his ability to overcome the handicaps genres naturally impose upon their users, is to gain an appreciation of his artistry in prose, an artistry matched by few of his pamphleteering contemporaries during the Civil War and Interregnum. As I shall attempt to demonstrate, Milton was capable of aesthetic accomplishment with his left hand as well as with his right.

"The Fitted Stile of Lofty,
Mean, or Lowly"

Areopagitica (1644) is a deliberative oration intended to promote liberty of conscience; *The Tenure of Kings and Magistrates* (1649) is a deliberative oration intended to promote political liberty.[31] They illustrate how Milton, as an advocate of Reformation, adapted classical rhetorical strategies to different needs. Both follow the oratorical structural model outlined in Cicero's *De Partitione Oratoria* and in Quintilian's *Institutio Oratoria*, each modifying the model according to its particular ends. Ciceronian maxims on the numerous functions of the high, middle, and low styles and the relationship of those styles to the texture of specific arguments guided Milton in both treatises. I shall examine the style of the exordium, the argument, and the peroration of each tract in order to show that Milton could accomplish in English prose what he had already accomplished in Latin. Although the rhetoric of *Areopagitica* and *The Tenure* grows out of the classical canons described in Chapter One, Milton's allegiance is far from blind. He found it necessary to transform his models so that he might present the case for liberty more effectively. Milton not only molded the high style of *Areopagitica* into a medium for expressing apocalyptic visions, but he made Ciceronian rhetoric serve the purposes of Christian prophecy in both orations. Another concern of this chapter will be to point out the ways in which *Areopagitica* and *The Tenure* develop from public and factual into personal and evocative. Finally, the analysis of two works five years apart — the only deliberative orations Milton composed during this period — will illuminate his changing conception of the oratorical mode. I shall argue that Milton progressed toward a species of oratory which relies upon the persuasive effects of Christian symbolism.

The style and argument of *Areopagitica* are closely integrated. Milton conceives of censorship as a dualistic concern intimately connected to the idea of temperance. Surely censorship is an immediate, practical political matter subject to repeal by the very parliamentarians who ordered it. Removing censorship would be equivalent to performing an act of temperance as Aristotle interpreted the virtue. For Aristotle, temperance was, of course, the

mean between extremes — in the case of *Areopagitica* between anarchy and authoritarian repression.[32] Moreover, repealing the
Order would be a fundamentally reasonable act, a restoration of
the ethical, intellectual, and political harmony which, Milton implies, was violated when the Order was imposed. Yet Milton
thought of censorship as more than a practical issue resolvable by
political means. In censorship he detected a symbolic menace
threatening to Reformation and to the concept of Christian temperance he held: choice of good with a full knowledge of evil.
Censorship could produce only a "fugitive and cloister'd vertue"
denied access to growth and fulfillment because it was unable to
perfect itself through trial. During the course of the oration Milton
looks carefully at the two sides of censorship. Stylistic variety
mirrors Milton's differing stances on the issue, while stylistic shifts
are often indicative of his change of focus from one aspect of the
dualism to the other. Style, then, has several functions in *Areopagitica*: it clarifies Milton's logical argument, emphasizes his pri-
orities of argument, and is itself a form of affective pleading.

Quintilian's definition of the nature and purpose of an exordium
(II, 486-90) fits Milton's procedure in *Areopagitica*: "The style of
the *exordium* should not resemble that of our purple patches nor
that of the argumentative and narrative portions of the speech, nor
yet should it be prolix or continuously ornate: it should rather seem
simple and unpremeditated. . . . For a method of pleading which
conceals its art and makes no vain display . . . will often be best
adapted to insinuate its way into the minds of its hearers."[33] The
exordium is a masterpiece of strategy which portrays Parliament
as a body of reasonable men capable of responding to a reasonable
proposition, although Milton knew that these very men had enacted licensing. He presents his case in the middle style, for he
could not risk alienating them with an emotional harangue in the
high style. His thesis is precise and direct: censorship is a political
issue resolvable through political action.

The tone of the exordium is modest and urbane in its advocacy
of the Aristotelian notion of temperance; licensing is an extreme
step which Parliament ought to reject in favor of more moderate,
reasoned measures of handling "unlicenc'd Printing." Milton's
subtlety in associating England and Athens makes his rhetorical
appeal witty rather than merely ingratiating. The middle style
with which he evokes the ideals of classical civilization is charac-
terized by schemes of repetition and redefinition instead of elaborate tropes. The effect of such schemes is to clarify and to focus
the reader's attention upon a significant argument; for example,

concerning the man who would speak out against censorship, Milton declares: "His highest praising is not flattery, and his plainest advice is a kinde of praising" (II, 488). Here the scheme *antimetabole*, akin to logical conversion, sharpens the distinction between praise and flattery by repeating the terms in converse order.

The bulk of *Areopagitica* develops Milton's case for freedom of the press, an argument which welds the narration, confirmation, and refutation into one structural unit. The opening volley of the pamphlet is in effect an historical narration. Censorship, Milton warns, was "invented by those whom we dislike and opposed by those whom we respect."[34] He divides the narrative into two sections, the first of which (II, 493-500) examines the question of censorship in classical times. Milton employs the low style of narration here to present examples from the intellectual history of the classical past which illustrate the use or abuse of reason on the issue of censorship. The behavior of the Spartans supports Milton's assertion that censorship is futile: they "took a slight occasion to chase *Archilochus* out of their City, perhaps for composing in a higher straine then their owne souldierly ballats and roundels could reach to" (II, 496). The poems of Archilochus "were suppressed in Sparta because of their licentiousness."[35] Euripides exposes the ironic foolishness of the Spartans when he notes that the Spartan life style itself was conducive to immorality. Censoring Archilochus' poems was hardly an effective way to prevent promiscuity since men and women "publicly performed gymnastic exercises together in the nude."[36]

In contrast to the betrayal of reason by the Spartans, the behavior of Cato the Censor exemplifies wisdom: "when *Carneades* and *Critolaus*, with the *Stoick Diogenes* comming Embassadors to *Rome*, tooke thereby occasion to give the City a tast of their Philosophy, they were suspected for seducers by no lesse a man then *Cato* the Censor, who mov'd it in the Senat to dismisse them speedily, and to banish all such *Attick* bablers out of *Italy*. But *Scipio* and others of the noblest Senators withstood him and his old *Sabin* austerity; honour'd and admir'd the men; and the Censor himself at last in his old age fell to the study of that whereof before hee was so scrupulous" (II, 497-98). Reason prevailed with Cato, who eventually came to respect and accept that which he had once feared. The examples of the Spartans and Cato represent Milton's analytical use of the classical context which had served as a means of evoking an ideal of wisdom in the exordium. The tone of the argument here, however, differs slightly from that of the exordium. In a plain style virtually devoid of schemes or tropes, Milton offers specimens of behavior which demand rational scrutiny. The reader is encouraged to interpret for himself the meaning, occasionally ironic, beneath the narrated events. The narrative persona remains unobtrusive, as he was in the exordium.

Unlike the first, the second phase of the narrative (II, 500-07) relies heavily upon pathetic appeal. Milton's sketch of the growth of censorship in Christian times implies that Rome devised it to impede Reformation. Because Milton wishes to link Rome with the type of repression currently in practice, he writes in the low style of satire, blending a logical proposition (Rome desires to hinder Reformation) with several kinds of pathetic proof. The following image epitomizes Milton's allegation that censorship is a satanic plot engineered by the Whore of Babylon ("mysterious iniquity") and her minion, the Pope: censorship "was never heard before, till that mysterious iniquity provokt and troubl'd at the first entrance of Reformation, sought out new limbo's and new hells wherein they might include our Books also within the number of their damned" (II, 506). His claim that censorship will interfere with Reformation makes explicit earlier suggestions and introduces what will become the culminating argument of the tract. The suspicion, fear, and hatred aroused by Milton's equation of censorship with the Inquisition is exploited by his sarcastic low diction and sardonic wit. He gleefully mocks the papal policy of assigning the Imprimatur only to books which were "approv'd and licenc't under the hands of 2 or 3 glutton Friers" (II, 503). Referring to the Imprimaturs he has quoted, Milton jibes: "Sure they have a conceit, if he of the bottomlesse pit had not long since broke prison, that this quadruple exorcism would barre him down" (II, 504).

In summary, the historical *narratio* sets forth a number of responses to the problem of censorship, and style shapes the reader's appraisal of those responses. Milton's analysis of classical reactions is objective, detached, at times ironic in tone. The low style of narration permits the reader to see for himself the admirably reasonable approach classical civilization took to the vexing issue. When Milton moves to Christian times, censorship is re-defined as a malevolent rather than a merely foolish practice, a threat to the exercise of Christian temperance, and the tone of the argument grows increasingly bitter and denunciatory. The persona's *ethos* becomes that of the satirist whose *saeva indignatio* is directed at those who in the past used censorship against Reformation and also, by implication, those who do so in the present. The classical low style of satire, with its vitriolic imagery, coarse diction, and caustic tone turns into a weapon in the hands of the Christian polemicist. Milton conceptualizes the issue of censorship in Christian terms. In the abhorred repression of the Inquisition may be seen a prefiguration of the ultimate result of censorship in England. Not only, then, does the movement from the low style of narration to the low style of satire parallel the thematic progression from a rational and practical conception of censorship to a visionary and apocalyptic one, but it implies a hierarchy of values as well. For Milton, the relevance of licensing to Reformation is paramount.

Like the historical argument, the climactic and lengthiest thesis of the oration breaks into two distinct parts.[37] Censorship, Milton insists, will loosen England's grip on the Christian truths it presently holds, and also delay the "reforming of Reformation" to which the nation has been called. After a brief analysis of the demeaning effects of censorship on learning and learned men (II, 541-43), an analysis which minimizes specifically Christian connotations, Milton explores in depth the link between tyranny over learning and tyranny over Reformation. His case rests upon a conception of Christian temperance as reasoned choice. Through the exercise of reason in differentiating good and evil and the exercise of will in choosing good, men respond to the demand of Providence that they retain the truth they possess. Three metaphoric narratives (II, 543-48) dramatize the dangers of censorship to the preservation of Christian truth. "There is not any burden," Milton charges, "that som would gladlier post off to another, then the charge and care of their Religion" (II, 543). A "wealthy man" already "addicted to his pleasure and to his profits" will discover in the stagnant environment of religious activity created by censorship an opportunity to "find himself out som factor, to whose care and credit he may commit the whole managing of his religious affairs; som Divine of note and estimation that must be" (II, 544). The implications of the argument are clear: censorship will encourage those enticed by the lure of worldly pleasures to uphold the external appearance of religion while neglecting its essence. Others will treat religion as a matter indifferent when they learn that "all things shall be order'd . . . nothing writt'n but what passes through the custom-house of certain Publicans that have the tunaging and the poundaging of all free spok'n truth" (II, 545). Finally, licensing will foster laxity and negligence among the clergy. Instead of preaching the Word, ministers will become idle speculators: "a *parochiall* Minister, who has his reward, and is at his *Hercules* pillars in a warm benefice, [will] be easily inclinable, if he have nothing else that may rouse up his studies, to finish his circuit in an English concordance and a *topic folio*" (II, 546).

Pathetic proof enters the argument by way of several comparisons and contrasts which polarize the reader's reactions. In opposition to the "Divine of note" who is "liberally supt," Milton places Christ, "whose morning appetite would have gladly fed on green figs between *Bethany* and *Jerusalem*" (II, 544). The simplicity of Christ emerges as the standard of judgment against which the reader is asked to measure the corruption of the worldly Divine. The idle speculation of the clergy stands condemned in the light of a minister's sacred obligations toward his flock: "it will concern him then to keep waking, to stand in watch, to set good guards and sentinells about his receiv'd opinions" (II, 547). The Christian warfare of truth necessitates that a minister remain fully informed of the ever-changing climate of theological opinion, lest he expose his parishioners to falsehood from any quarter.

Milton's argument that censorship and stagnation are synonymous is presented in the middle style. Rather than contending with strict logic that censorship will erode religious belief, he relies upon the suggestive value of the three metaphoric narratives, permitting the reader to perceive the juxtapositions of truth and falsehood they embody. The urgent tone of the argument is heightened by the persona's creation of a dramatic immediacy through repeated exhortations to Parliament to apprehend the dangers to Reformation imminent in licensing. Drawing upon the fear he has aroused over the effects of the Order, Milton's exhortations frequently utilize schemes of repetition and arrangement for emphasis:

> For if we be sure we are in the right, and doe not hold the truth guiltily, which becomes not, if we our selves condemn not our own weak and frivolous teaching, and the people for an untaught and irreligious gadding rout, what can be more fair, then when a man judicious, learned, and of a conscience, for ought we know, as good as theirs that taught us what we know, shall not privily from house to house, which is more dangerous, but openly by writing publish to the world what his opinion is, what his reasons, and wherefore that which is now thought cannot be sound. (II, 547-48)

Careful reiteration by means of *anaphora* ("if we . . . if we; what his . . . what his") and a rhythmical smoothness brought about by *isocolon, parison,* and ellipsis convey Milton's message more effectively than naked logic could have done. In the middle style of impassioned argument, then, Milton cautions the reader about the pitfalls of moral stagnation and regression. Implicit in his warning is a pivotal conception of Christian temperance: standing and waiting. To live the Christian life faithfully and vigilantly is to perform an act of temperance.

The heightened style and reliance upon metaphor evident in the preceding argument culminate in Milton's final appeal: censorship "hinders and retards the importation of our richest Marchandize, Truth" (II, 548-68). That appeal, including the mislabeled "national digression,"[38] is unified by a visionary rhetoric which equates the truth of Reformation with the nation's destiny and the conspiracy of licensing with antichristian malice. Milton pleads in the high style, a style whose apocalyptic character represents the adaptation of classical theory to his needs as a Christian orator. He structures the argument as an allegorical narrative in which England is joined with Zion and singled out as a nation in historical time engaged in Christian warfare to defend Christ's Church from its enemies. For the Christian orator, the abundant metaphor Cicero and Quintilian advised for the high style has become apocalyptic metaphor. Christian temperance, which had earlier been associated with the preservation of truth, is now identified as a way of enlarging that truth. The exercise of reason and free will constitutes a national response to the Providential call for England to lead the Reformed Church.

Milton begins the narrative by proclaiming that although England has been blessed with truth, truth has been "scatter'd" by God's enemies, a contention he illustrates by alluding to the myth of Isis and Osiris:

> . . . as that story goes of the *AEgyptian Typhon* with his conspirators, how they dealt with the good *Osiris*, took the virgin Truth, hewd her lovely form into a thousand peeces, and scatter'd them to the four winds. From that time ever since, the sad friends of Truth, such as durst appear, imitating the carefull search that *Isis* made for the mangl'd body of *Osiris*, went up and down gathering up limb by limb still as they could find them. We have not yet found them all, Lords and Commons, nor ever shall doe, till her Masters second comming; he shall bring together every joynt and member, and shall mould them into an immortall feature of lovelines and perfection. (II, 549)

The legend of Osiris merges with the Second Coming of Christ to foreshadow England's destiny. The search for truth must not be abandoned until the "dissever'd peeces which are yet wanting to the body of Truth" are recovered. Only by allowing those who are falsely branded "schisms and sects" to continue that search can England realize its destiny as leader of Reformation.

Now, Milton affirms, "God is decreeing to begin some new and great period in his Church, ev'n to the reforming of Reformation it self: what does he then but reveal Himself to his servants, and as his manner is, first to his English-men" (II, 553). The "reforming of Reformation," equivalent to joining together every "joynt and member" of the body of Truth, cannot proceed unless "there be pens and heads there, sitting by their studious lamps, musing, searching, revolving new notions and idea's wherewith to present, as with their homage and their fealty the approaching Reformation" (II, 554). The pen is truly an instrument of the Lord, as are those who wield it. Yet God's work is not easily perceivable to the eyes of men; England must be wary of what it licenses "for opinion in good men is but knowledge in the making. Under these fantastic terrors of sect and schism, we wrong the earnest and zealous thirst after knowledge and understanding which God hath stirr'd up" (II, 554). Milton's vision of Christian temperance turns "opinion" into a means of discovering truth. In apocalyptic terms, those who might be condemned as sectaries are ironically transformed into the potential leaders of the nation.

The intellectual polarities inherent in Milton's apocalyptic rhetoric take the form of archetypal images and allusions which eulogize those who forge England's destiny and damn those who would impede it. Like the Israelites in the desert, England is guided in its struggle to gather the limbs of Osiris by the "blaze that *Zuinglius* and *Calvin* hath beacon'd up" (II, 550). The spiritual truth symbolized by the "light" of the fathers of Reformation will act as armor to shield England from Reformation's foes. Milton converts the search for truth into a symbol of Christian warfare which will unify the nation, and London into a metaphoric "City of refuge, the mansion house of liberty, encompast and surrounded with [God's] protection; the shop of warre hath not there more anvils and hammers waking, to fashion out the plates and instruments of armed Justice in defence of beleaguer'd Truth, then there be pens and heads there" (II, 553-54). The warfare of the pen is looked upon favorably by a "great and worthy stranger" who, in the metaphoric context of Milton's argument, might be identified with Christ, leader of the Militant Church: "I doubt not, if some great and worthy stranger should come among us, wise to discern the mould and temper of a people . . . observing the high hopes and aims, the diligent alacrity of our extended thoughts and reasonings in the pursuance of truth and freedom, but that he would cry out as *Pirrhus* did, admiring the Roman docility and courage, if such were my *Epirots,* I would not despair the greatest design that could be attempted to make a Church or Kingdom happy" (II, 554-55). When the "City of refuge" is "as it were besieg'd and blockt about, her navigable river infested . . . defiance and battell oft rumor'd to be marching up ev'n to her walls" (II, 556-57), "reading, inventing, discoursing" in the pursuit of truth may be seen as a "lively and cherfull presage of our happy successe and victory."

In the apocalyptic style, time present and time future, literal fact and metaphoric meaning combine to prefigure the ultimate result of England's efforts to translate the truths of Reformation into practice. The events of the Civil War which raged as Milton wrote the oration are elevated into symbols of Christian warfare in which the pen replaces the cannon. The apocalyptic persona builds classical concepts of ethical proof into the theological framework of the argument. The orator has become a Christian prophet who, in urging England to lead the completion of Reformation, stands forth as an emblem of zealous righteousness which Parliament and the entire nation would do well to imitate. We have noted the prophet's celebration of the perfection England might attain in future time. He calls as well for the eradication of censorship in the present time, for truth and falsehood are irreconcilable. Licensing, the prophet warns, is a plot which "was first establisht and put in practice by Antichristian malice and mystery on set purpose to extinguish, if it were possible, the light of Reformation, and to settle falshood" (II, 548). He banishes the advocates of censorship to a nether region of demonic darkness and ignorance. Only a "grosse conforming stupidity, a stark and dead congealment of *wood and hay and stubble* forc't and frozen together" (II, 564) can follow upon the repression of truth. These images of congealment and stagnation are the antitheses of the "light" of wisdom. The "pride and ignorance" of those who champion licensing have made them dupes of the satanic "adversarie" who awaits the hour when the faithful have "brancht themselves out" (II, 556) so that he can destroy them.

As we have observed, Milton's most extensive and eloquent call for the repeal of censorship evokes a response within the spirit to England's destiny as leader of Reformation. Pathetic proof directed at the utopian yearnings of the Puritan spiritual temperament dominates that call. The apocalyptic high style transcends reason, drawing its strength instead from fundamental Christian beliefs. As did the narrative argument, Milton's final plea gradually develops into a conceptualization of censorship in terms of Reformation, and again stylistic progression underlines his hierarchy of values. Holding fast to the truths one has inherited is admirable, but even more praiseworthy is the heroic struggle to enlarge those truths.

Like the preceding sections of *Areopagitica*, the peroration (II, 568-70) generally follows classical stylistic precepts. Both Quintilian and Cicero had recommended that the peroration recapitulate the argument, amplifying its most important phases to stir the minds of the readers.[39] Accordingly, Milton reiterates his central thesis: licensing will block the advance of Reformation by stifling religious truth. Rather than risk prohibiting wisdom in an attempt to prohibit folly, England must recognize one essential fact: truth may "have more shapes then one." Moreover, "such is the order of Gods enlightning his Church, to dispense and deal out by degrees his beam, so as our earthly eyes may best sustain it" (II, 566). To plead his case Milton selects the ornate metaphoric style classical rhetoricians had deemed appropriate to the peroration, again modifying classical rules by appending to the style an apocalyptic tone and significant amounts of Biblical allusion and imagery. These Christian qualities are evident in his assessment of the debilitating effect of censorship on truth: "then rather she turns herself into all shapes, except her own, and perhaps tunes her voice according to the time, as *Micaiah* did before *Ahab*" (II, 563). Attempting to polarize the reader's reactions, Milton refers to the negative symbols of Roman Catholic and Anglican ritual: "I fear yet this iron yoke of outward conformity hath left a slavish print upon our necks; the ghost of a linnen decency yet haunts us" (II, 563-64). Laudian "decency" is a strong pathetic reminder of an earlier plot to enforce "uniformity" of religion.[40] The ornate style of the peroration is marked, finally, by a profusion of verbal schemes and rhythmic devices contributing to a euphonious effect: "When a man hath bin labouring the hardest labour in the deep mines of knowledge, hath furnisht out his findings in all their equipage, drawn forth his reasons as it were a battell raung'd, scatter'd and defeated all objections in his way . . ." (II, 562). Built around the metaphors of mining and battle, the sentence achieves a rhythmic harmony through alliteration, *anaphora*, and *diazeugma* ("furnisht . . . drawn . . . scatter'd").

Yet the rhetorical appeal of the peroration does not depend entirely upon a high style rich in pathetic proof, for Milton's conclusion echoes the complex, dualistic character of the *Areopagitica* itself. Running through the peroration is a plainer style whose primary thrust is logical and which asserts that Parliament, in complete control of licensing, can take immediate, practical steps to eliminate a harmful law. If his premises have become evident, Milton contends, they will inspire the legislature to take the only reasonable course of action available: "For this *authentic* Spanish policy of licencing books, if I have said ought, will prove the most unlicenc't book it self within a short while" (II, 569).

Stylistic fusion in the peroration thus implies Milton's integration of the thematic duality which had prevailed throughout the tract. With the apocalyptic style we are reminded of the overriding Christian significance of licensing. Linked throughout *Areopagitica* with the rational, pragmatic side of the issue, the plain style suggests that an unwise political edict can be repealed without great difficulty. Time present and time future, the visionary and the practical are brought together. Repealing censorship would surely restore the intellectual harmony presumably violated when it was enacted. More importantly, a repeal would be in accordance with the mandate of Providence and would safeguard the nation's right to perform acts of Christian temperance in time future.

II

The Scriptural paradigm for Reformation to which Milton referred in the apocalyptic high style of *Areopagitica* becomes a comprehensive frame of reference in *The Tenure of Kings and Magistrates*. Augustine's premise that the ecclesiastical orator's "strength is derived from a source deeper than human skill"[41] explains the eloquence of *The Tenure*. Since the verities of Scripture are eminently persuasive, the Christian orator need not rely upon imagistic flourish or passionate flights in the high style; rhetorical artifice might, in fact, obscure the very truth he sought to illuminate. The evocative eloquence of Christian symbols, not ingenious arguments or stylistic display, persuades the reader of *The Tenure*. From virtually the opening lines of the pamphlet we are caught up in the Augustinian Rhetoric of Silence,[42] a pervasive movement from literal to symbolic. Milton's oratory, drawing upon the principles of Augustinian exegesis, leads the reader to apprehend the eternal and the temporal as intrinsically unified and mutually illuminating so that contemporary reality may be interpreted in relation to a final meaning. His appeals to logic and to classical authorities, evident throughout the tract, conflict in no way with the body of Scriptural references I shall examine. However, biblical and Christian allusions are the principal cohesive elements of *The Tenure*; they unify Milton's style, tone, and thematic concerns.

Milton's exegesis in *The Tenure* follows from the premise that specific historical events and persons have Scriptural precedents which ought to be of profound import for a Protestant nation.[43] The voice of Scripture rings loud and clear in the monarchial crisis of 1649. The exordium (III, 190-97) of *The Tenure* introduces one of Milton's major themes by branding the Presbyterians as "those *That doe the worke of the Lord negligently*."[44] Although the Presbyterians have "bandied and born armes against thir King, devested him, disannointed him," they now "lay the staine of disloyaltie, and worse, on those proceedings, which are the necessary consequences of thir own former actions" (III, 191). Milton's accusation is supported by biblical allusions which associate the Presbyterians with symbols of evil. The "mercy" of the Presbyterians "is the mercy of wicked men; and their mercies, wee read are cruelties;[45] hazarding the welfare of a whole Nation, to have sav'd one, whom so oft they have tearm'd *Agag*;[46] and vilifying the blood of many *Jonathans*[47] that have sav'd *Israel*" (III, 193-94). Proverbs reveals the duplicity of the Presbyterians, while the story from Samuel dramatizes the effect of "mercy" which is in reality cruelty. By calling for mercy toward Charles (Agag) the Presbyterians risk the renewal of a tyranny hostile to Reformation and condemn those Jonathans (both Presbyterians and Independents) who have attempted to save the nation.

Presbyterian malevolence is likewise evident in their deliberate distortion of Scripture, their equation of those who oppose them with rebels against proper theocratic government: "to bring Delinquents [such as King Charles] without exemption to a faire Tribunal by the common National Law against murder, is now to be no less than *Corah, Dathan,* and *Abiram*" (III, 196-97).[48] Milton reminds us that while the Presbyterians compare their rule to that of Moses and Aaron, their political scheming likens them to "*Corah, Dathan,* and *Abiram*." Just as Scripture provides symbols of the evil hypocrisy of the Presbyterians, unmasking their deception, it also implies that they must inevitably face "the tryal of Justice, which is the Sword of God" because they have failed the Lord in refusing to execute the King.

The exordium of the tract is written in the middle style of impassioned argument. Logic shares the stage with denunciation as

Milton tries to convince the reader of the link between Scripture and contemporary history. A movement toward order and definition appears, for example, in his explanation of the attitudes productive of either liberty or tyranny: "For indeed none can love freedom heartilie, but good men; the rest love not freedom, but licence; which never hath more scope or more indulgence then under Tyrants" (III, 190). The logical division in the sentence is paralleled by schematic antithesis and emphasized by curt-Senecan phrasing. Later in the exordium logic yields to vehemence when Milton attacks the Presbyterians: "For while the hope to bee made Classic and Provincial Lords led them on, while pluralities greas'd them thick and deep, to the shame and scandal of Religion . . . to fight against the Kings person . . . was good, was lawfull, was no resisting of Superior powers" (III, 196). Unlike the austerity of the lines cited above, this passage drives home its satiric message with schemes of repetition such as *anaphora* ("while . . . while; was . . . was . . . was"), alliteration, and satiric, affective diction. The dualistic thrust of the middle style sets up symbolic associations which will reverberate through the tract.

In the exordium Milton follows the oratorical mandate to instruct, by first singling out and then castigating those who do the work of the Lord negligently. Ethical appeal derives in part from an assumption of Presbyterian "wickedness,"[49] but primarily from Milton's own zealous indignation at flagrant denials of the divine will. In his persona we witness a type of response to Providential edict; his example exhorts others to examine the Scriptures with care, to look beyond the political struggles of 1649 to the emblematic struggle of righteousness and iniquity in which all of England participates. The battle with Antichrist is at hand.

Relying upon Scriptural paradigm and the paradigm of Christian history, the argument of *The Tenure* draws out the implications of the exordium. Through "examples" which "ought to have most waight with us" Milton sketches a symbolic pattern rich in evocative significance. The exordium had urged that a tyrant be punished and the confirmation (III, 212-22) defines the method: "Among the Jews this custom of tyrant-killing was not unusual. First *Ehud*, a man whom God had raysd to deliver Israel from *Eglon* King of *Moab*, who had conquerd and rul'd over them eighteene years, being sent to him as an Ambassador with a present, slew him in his own house"[50] (III, 213). In explicating the symbolic events of the confirmation Milton is careful to refute any objections that Scripture does not provide guidance in the present crisis. To those who protest that Eglon was a foreign invader, not an Israelite, Milton answers "no Prince so native but professes to hold by Law" (III, 213). When Eglon and Charles abused the power of kingship each became deserving of punishment, and Milton allows the reader to perceive the imperative that Charles must be killed just as Eglon was.

The Scriptural example of Jehu and Jehoram denies the claim that royal sovereignty forbids a subject's rising up against his king: "And whereas *Jehu* had special command to slay *Jehoram* a successive and hereditarie Tyrant, it seems not the less imitable for that. . . . Nor is it likely that God who had so many wayes of punishing the house of *Ahab* would have sent a subject against his Prince, if the fact in it self, as don to a Tyrant, had bin of bad example"[51] (III, 215-16). Milton's assertion that God would not permit a misleading example leaves the reader at liberty to equate present and Scriptural time and therefore to discover repeated and irrevocable Scriptural precedent for the tyranny of Charles.[52] The Old Testament exempla of the confirmation evoke the inexorable, dispassionate Justice of Jehovah: None who sins will escape punishment, for the anger of Jehovah at evildoers must exact a full measure of retribution.

Approaching present history, Milton passes to Christian times and explains Christ's attitude toward tyrants:

> [Christ] declares his mind not obscurely; accounting thir absolute autority no better then Gentilism, yea though they flourish'd it over with the splendid name of Benefactors; charging those that would be his Disciples to usurp no such dominion . . . . And although hee himself were the meekest, and came on earth to be so, yet to a Tyrant we hear him not voutsafe an humble word: But *Tell that Fox, Luc.* 13. (III, 217)

Christ's pronouncements, especially his warning to King Herod (*"Tell that Fox"*), are consistent with those of the Old Testament; tyrants are not to be tolerated. The words of Christ possess an evocative value different from, but complementary to, Milton's earlier references to Old Testament texts. Christ's compassion for his spiritual subjects will not permit them to be oppressed by a temporal ruler. Moreover, Christ instructed his followers to allow neither king nor kingdom to hold sway over the commonwealth of the spirit.

The historical examples which Milton now cites, taken largely from the British past, imply that divine and human time constitute a continuum. Hence: "No marvel then if since the faith of Christ

[was] receav'd, in purer or impurer times, to depose a King and put him to death for Tyranny, hath bin accounted . . . just and requisite" (III, 217-18). In effect, nations and individuals who refuse to endure a tyrant "doe the worke of the Lord," becoming emblems of obedient response to Scriptural edict. The punishment of an unjust ruler is, in fact, a sacred act by which man may shape temporal events in accordance with the Providential design. Christian Britain assumes in this context a singular significance as a nation which has ever sought to fulfill the wishes of Providence. With these nationalistic allusions Milton evokes the unbroken British tradition of faithful service to God.

The refutation (III, 222-27) enlarges the pattern of Providential history emerging in the confirmation. In gathering "examples . . . chiefly Presbyterian" against those who "have writt'n that the proceedings now in Parlament against the King, are without precedent from any Protestant State or Kingdom," Milton appeals to the Providential sense of destiny deeply rooted in the Puritan consciousness. The Puritan's concept of identity as one of God's elite necessitated that he attach a special importance to the historical events which followed the Reformation. The hand of God was manifest in the spread of Reformation, virtually assuring that zealous Protestants might read the history of Reformation in emblematic terms with a certainty that the will of God would be manifested to his people. The evocative appeal of the refutation stems from this Puritan self-consciousness and zeal, zeal which had already been operative in the overthrow of episcopacy and the defeat of Charles.

Milton devotes most of his refutation to an explication of John Knox's arguments that the Scotch depose Queen Mary. The actions of Scotland witness the consistency of Reformed Christian history with the grand paradigm. "In the yeare 1564," Milton writes:

> *John Knox* a most famous Divine and the reformer of *Scotland* to the Presbyterian discipline, at a general Assembly maintained op'nly in a dispute against *Lethington* the Secretary of State, that Subjects might and ought execute Gods judgements upon thir King; that the fact of *Jehu* and others against thir King having the ground of Gods ordinary command to put such and such offenders to death was not extraordinary, but to bee imitated of all that preferr'd the honour of God to the affection of flesh and wicked Princes.
> (III, 223-24)

Lest the significance of Knox's proclamation pass unnoticed, Milton affirms that the Scottish rebellion is of emblematic value, "as if they labourd to inform us what wee were to doe, and what they intended upon the like occasion" (III, 225). If Knox's denunciation is paradigmatic, so is the fate of Queen Mary: "three years after, [the rebels] met in the feild *Mary* thir lawful and hereditary Queen, took her prisoner . . . and the same yeare depos'd her" (III, 225). True, the Scots did not execute Mary, but they apologized "that they had us'd toward her more lenity then shee deserv'd, that thir Ancestors had heretofore punish'd thir Kings by death or banishment" (III, 225). Knox's plea for the prosecution of God's Justice transforms the deposition of Mary into an act of zeal in accordance with Providential design; Mary's fate is an historical prefiguration of the Lord's guidance of the Reformed Church. Charles' execution will likewise become an emblematic event in the history of Reformation, and the English people sanctified instruments in the hands of Providence. The climactic example of Scotland defines in unmistakable terms England's response to the divine imperative.

The examples which dot the confirmation and refutation are presented in the low style of argument. Yet in the metaphoric context of *The Tenure* Milton's style is more than a mere tool of the logician. It is a transparent medium for symbolic discourse; we pierce through Milton's words to a higher level of meaning. His plainness facilitates the literal-to-symbolic movement of the oration by pointing up the unity of Scriptural and temporal history, divine and human time. It instructs by avoiding elaborate imagery and rhetorical flourish, thereby shaping the reader's perspective so that he concentrates upon the truth of Christian paradigm. Although the reader must reason out the argumentative analogies Milton occasionally offers,[53] logic in itself is only a transitional step, and not the essence of Milton's appeals. We are persuaded, rather, by the eloquence of Scriptural precept and human response to it. The literal plainness of the style is reenforced by schemes of repetition which serve to re-define Milton's theses. Hence he draws a thematic parallel which is supported by structural parallelism and heightened by *anaphora* and *isocolon*: "For look how much right the King of *Spaine* hath to govern us at all, so much right hath the King of *England* to govern us tyrannically" (III, 214).

The peroration (III, 227-43) of *The Tenure* recalls the dilemma which Milton had outlined in the exordium: "backsliders" among the Presbyterians refuse to "doe the worke of the Lord." Clearly the Presbyterians have deposed King Charles *de facto*: "Have they not utterly broke the Oath of Allegeance, rejecting the Kings command and autority sent them from any part of the Kingdom whether in things lawful or unlawful? Have they not abjur'd the Oath of Supremacy by setting up the Parlament without the King" (III, 228-29). But now they balk at executing him, denying the command of Scripture and the precedent of other Reformed states. In doing the work of the Lord negligently, the Presbyterians have cast their lot with Antichrist, with evil, meriting Milton's attack upon their "clov'n tongues of falshood and dissention" and their "fals prophecies." Rather than trusting hypocritical leaders, England must follow the dictates of Scripture: "as God was heretofore angry with the Jews who rejected him and his forme of Goverment to choose a King . . . he will bless us, and be propitious to us who reject a King to make him onely our leader and supreme governour in the conformity as neer as may be of his own ancient goverment; if we have at least but so much worth in us to entertaine the sense of our future happiness, and the courage to receave what God voutsafes us" (III, 236). Divine wisdom and the practice of other Protestant states offer a more viable means of dealing with political chaos than does the behavior of the Presbyterians.

In the peroration the middle style impels the reader to adopt the course of action which Milton's argument had clarified for him. The evocative force of the peroration stems from Milton's assertion of his prophetic mandate in the form of denunciation and eulogy. His exemplary voice articulates a type of response to the political turmoil he had earlier described. Repeatedly, he lashes out at Presbyterian falsehood: "If then thir Oaths of subjection brok'n, new Supremacy obey'd, new Oaths and Covnants tak'n, notwithstanding frivolous evasions, have in plaine termes unking'd the King, much more then hath thir sev'n years Warr not depos'd him onely, but outlaw'd him, and defi'd him" (III, 230). At the outset of the peroration, there are numerous analogues to the above example, especially in the series of rhetorical questions or *percontatio* which Milton directs to the Presbyterians: ". . . have not they . . ." Milton's polemic stigmatizes the Presbyterians as the minions of Antichrist, bent on the perversion of Scripture and Reformation. The orator has become a Jeremiac prophet who hurls the divine wrath at them.

Invective defers to optimism as the synthesis which Milton forges in the peroration takes shape. The middle style which had elicited hatred of the Presbyterians now serves to eulogize the

path of enlightenment which England must follow to achieve political harmony: "But God, as we have cause to trust . . . from the
murmurs of new discord will incline [the people] to heark'n rather
with erected minds to the voice of our Supreme Magistracy [Par-
liament], calling us to liberty and the flourishing deeds of a reformed Common-wealth" (III, 236). The utopian rhetoric of the
passage exhorts all to seek the "reforming of Reformation" and
celebrates the ideals which the Presbyterians threaten. In the act
of proclaiming the benevolence of Providence the orator's voice has
acquired an apocalyptic timbre.

In his final appeal to the Presbyterians, both laymen and divines,
Milton juxtaposes the alternatives of action which will either
assist or hinder England's progress toward Reformation, so that
the middle style combines the functions of denunciation and eulogy
it had performed earlier. Hence, he asks the divines to embrace
again the Scriptural ideals of the ministry:

> Let them assemble in Consistory with thir Elders and Dea-
> cons, according to ancient Ecclesiastical rule, to the preserv-
> ing of Church-discipline, each in his several charge, and not
> a pack of Clergiemen by themselves to belly-cheare in thir
> presumptuous Sion, or to promote designes, abuse and gull
> the simple Laity, and stir up tumult, as the Prelats did, for
> the maintenance of thir pride and avarice. (III, 241-42)

The style of these lines enacts in microcosm the dichotomies between divine truth and human folly, harmony and chaos which
have permeated *The Tenure*. At the outset of the sentence Milton
clarifies the role the ministers ought to play in the present political
crisis, and his style is accordingly logical and precise. As the sentence progresses, satiric elements enter in the form of accusations
phrased harshly. The salvific wisdom of Scriptural precept contrasts with the dark vision of human corruption, proclaiming
emphatically the manner in which divines, and all of England, may
"doe the work of the Lord."

As I have demonstrated, Milton, who had at his command the
full range of oratorical styles and strategies, transformed classical
guidelines when they failed to serve his needs as a Christian orator.
In both *Areopagitica* and *The Tenure* may be observed, moreover,
the gradual but consistent progression — in individual arguments
and in the pamphlets as a whole — away from logic and the formal
strictures of classical rhetoric toward the evocative context of
Christian apocalypse. Milton devotes the final argument of *Areopagitica* and the lengthy peroration of *The Tenure* to a prophetic

appraisal in Christian terms of the issues which had concerned him in each work. Milton's prophetic overview, an assessment presented in language uniquely his own, represents the culmination of his efforts to translate the literal and factual into the imaginative and affective, and to delineate an idealized response to matters of importance for Reformation. Differing approaches to rhetoric and style in the two orations point to Milton's changing conception of the oratorical mode. Milton moved from Christian imagery in *Areopagitica* to Christian symbolism in *The Tenure*. By utilizing the affective context of Scripture throughout *The Tenure*, he achieved virtually the same persuasive effect he had achieved with the apocalyptic high style of *Areopagitica*, for the eloquence of Scripture itself rendered superfluous much of the rhetorical apparatus thought essential by Cicero and Quintilian. Thus in *The Tenure* Milton is less in evidence as an orator skilled in the devices of classical rhetoric than he is as an exemplum of regenerate response to Providential design.

From History to Oratory

The oratorical mode again served Milton well when he composed the *History of Britain*. Milton's practices as a historian were guided by the Augustinian philosophy of history which held that the moral evaluation of facts must take precedence over the mere recording of them. In order to transcribe accurately the events of Britain's past, Milton consistently employs a logical methodology and a plain, tonally neutral style. While his function as a recorder of facts remains static, Milton's role as a moral evaluator steadily increases in complexity. Oratorical techniques and styles are the means whereby he persuades the reader that any nation's political freedom is contingent upon its spiritual freedom. Like an epideictic orator, he praises exemplary moral behavior on the few occasions when it appears and, more often, indicts in a "searching stile" of satire the degeneracy of the Britons and Saxons. However, in the final two books of the *History*, satiric vehemence is frequently displaced by weariness and resignation. Milton has been forced by history itself to concede that backsliding is the destiny of postlapsarian mankind.

In part because of Milton's own apparent disavowals of the orator's art in the *History*, evidence of such art has not been sought. Milton's unequivocal condemnation in *The Reason of Church-Government* (I, 812) of monkish historians whose superstition and bias detracted from their objectivity as record keepers adumbrates his own commitment to rectify such errors, errors which had made England's "noble" achievements "small." His remark in the *History* itself that he included details from Britain's Roman past in order to avoid "an unsightly gap so neer to the beginning" (V, 41) seems to verify that commitment. Such "an unsightly gap" would leave him vulnerable to the same retorts he had hurled at his monkish predecessors. Moreover, Milton's comments on the rhetorical methodology proper to historical writing remove any doubt that he valued the judicious gathering of facts: "I do not insist on ornate language; I ask for a historian, not an orator. Nor would I favor injecting frequent maxims or judgments on historical exploits, lest by breaking the chain of events, the historian invade the province of the political writer; *if, in explaining plans and narrating deeds, he follows to the best of his ability not his own invention or conjecture but the truth, he truly fulfills his function*"

(VII, 501; my italics). A search for the rhetorical trappings Milton repudiates above meets with little success, for set speeches, numerous digressions, and the ornate style are indeed rare.[54]

Yet Milton's claim that his *History* ought to "instruct and benefit them that read" (V, 4), as well as "redound to [God's] glory and the good of the *British* Nation" cannot be discounted, pointing as it does to a didactic intention consonant with the humanist tradition.[55] French Fogle has stated emphatically and convincingly the case for Milton's didacticism in the *History*: "From classical writers he took his ideas and his models for the manner and style of writing history; and from his Christian background he derived the purpose of history, which was to show the working of Providence in human affairs; *and from both sources he drew the notion that the prime end of history was instruction, whether in statecraft, in a knowledge of human motives in action, or in morality.*"[56] Elsewhere (V, xx-xxv) Fogle traces Milton's access to the documents which saw in history a wealth of examples to instruct and inspire. Michael Landon's observation that Milton avoids the whole "Renaissance scientific approach" with its scrutinizing of astrology, climate, and racial characteristics bolsters Fogle's case indirectly.[57] What seems clear from this critical controversy is that, like other late Renaissance histories, Milton's is a "compound of piety and research, moralism and realism, Christianity and classicism."[58]

Milton's purpose in the *History* is in fact dualistic — to record facts and to evaluate them. The Christian view of history propounded by Augustine resolves the contradictions seemingly inherent in such a dualism. Augustine visualized history as a body of evidence verifying repeated Providential intervention in the affairs of mankind. Before he approaches the historical particulars in which it is embodied, the Christian historian has an overview of the Providential plan in mind.[59] Augustine cautioned the historian against lapsing into factual inaccuracies, for he fully expected that facts would bear mute witness to the gradual unfolding of God's design. Although minute historical particulars might prove difficult to comprehend, the Christian historian could rest content that his readers would discern in the data as a whole a foreordained pattern. If, however, the facts at his disposal appeared either to obscure or to contradict the Providential plan, the historian was free to bring them into harmony with it, since, in Augustine's mind, the moral ramifications of facts outweighed the facts themselves.[60] In effect, factual precision could be dispensed with if a situation forced the historian to choose between piety and accuracy.

Milton did, as Fogle argues, "fix the past within a meaningful pattern of his own devising,"[61] one directly related to the master theme of liberty. As Milton stated in the Digression, "the gaining or loosing of libertie is the greatest change to better or to worse that may befall a nation under civil goverment" (V, 441). The Britons and Saxons, Milton leads us to believe, forfeited their liberty through moral corruption, bringing down upon themselves the chastisement of retributive justice: "And by the customary judgment and, so to speak, just retaliation of God, it happens that a nation which cannot rule and govern itself, but has delivered itself into slavery to its own lusts, is enslaved also to other masters whom it does not choose" (IV, 684). The validity of this moral paradigm of internal and external slavery reaches out of the shadowy past which Milton brings to light in the *History* and touches seventeenth-century Britain. I would suggest that Milton's primary rationale for compiling the *History* was to "raise a knowledg . . . both great and weighty" (V, 130) of this ominous axiom so that the mistakes of the past might not be repeated anew. Should Englishmen be able to profit from the transgressions of their ancestors, they would strengthen their hold on the moral worthiness which had thus far distinguished them as leaders of Reformation.

Without an accurate recording of the past, free from exaggerations and distortions, however, the homiletic import of the tract would be considerably diminished. To insure that, insofar as possible, his moral strictures rest on a bedrock of factual certainty, Milton strives consistently to fulfill his role as judicious recorder of British history. That role consists of three basic responsibilities, the first of which is to strip away from facts the mythological accretions built up over the centuries. Milton's dissection of the legendary King Arthur is a case in point. To prove Arthur was "more renown'd in Songs and Romances" than in reality he attacks the primary sources of the Arthurian myth. Our information about Arthur, Milton reports, derives principally from

> *Nennius*, a very trivial writer[62] yet extant. . . . Or out of a *British* Book *[Historia Regum Britaniae]*, the same which he of *Monmouth* set forth, utterly unknown to the World, till more then 600 years after the dayes of *Arthur*, of whom (as *Sigebert* in his Chronicle confesses) all other Histories were silent, both Foren and Domestic, except only that fabulous Book. (V, 165-66)

His appeal is to logical probability. Clearly, the validity of Arthur's exploits is subject to serious question when one realizes that Malmesbury and other popularizers of Arthur have merely parroted the uncertain conclusions of Nennius, conclusions about which Malmesbury himself expressed skepticism.[63] Moreover, the *Historia* of Monmouth, recorded so long after Arthur's death, would very likely contain sizeable inaccuracies.[64] Nor can the reader verify Monmouth's verdict by consulting other contemporary sources, for such sources are silent on the subject. Skepticism is the only plausible verdict, not only in this instance, but in Milton's later juxtaposition of Arthur's legendary feats to a known fact about him: *"Melvas* King of that Country which is now *Summerset,* kept from [Arthur] *Gueniver* his Wife a whole year in the Town of *Glaston,* and restor'd her at the entreaty of *Gildas,* rather then for any enforcement, that *Artur* with all his Chivalry could make against a small Town defended only by a moory situation" (V, 166-67). One must agree with Milton's subsequent logical conclusion, inherent in the facts, that ineptitude of this sort is hardly proof of legendary valor. In effect, Milton's critique of Arthur is a scholarly one supported by ample marginalia which the reader may examine. This factual evidence, together with the impeccable logic Milton applies to it, moves us to second his decision not "furder to contest about such uncertainties" (V, 171).

When reliable facts apparently conflict or when his sources are unmistakably in error, Milton will intervene to remedy matters, as he does here:

> *Ethelwolf* the Son of *Ecbert* succeeded, by *Malmsbury* describ'd a man of mild nature, not inclin'd to War, or delighted with much Dominion; that therfore contented with the antient *West-Saxon* bounds, he gave to *Ethelstan* his Brother, or Son, as some write, the Kingdome of *Kent* and *Essex. But the Saxon Annalist, whose Autority is Elder, saith plainly, that both these Countries and Sussex, were bequeath'd to Ethelstan by Ecbert his Father.* (V, 261; my italics in ll. 6-8)

Again Milton invokes logical probability: an authority generally reliable will likely be so in a specific instance. We are not asked to accept Milton's judgment on faith, since we may consult the same texts he did. If Milton is fortunate enough to have a trusted source at hand, he is often satisfied simply to transcribe details directly from it. For his account of the Roman invasion of Britain, Milton relies heavily upon Caesar's *Commentaries*, from which the following summary of a Roman misfortune principally comes:

> *Caesar* at this news [that almost all his Ships in a Tempest that night had suffer'd wrack] recalls his Legions, himself in all hast riding back to the Sea-side, beheld with his own Eyes the ruinous prospect. About forty Vessels were sunk and lost, the residue so torn, and shak'n as not to be new rigg'd without much labour. Strait he assembles what number of Ship-wrights either in his own Legions or from beyond Sea, could be summon'd; appoints *Labienus* on the *Belgian* side to build more; and with a dreadful industry of ten days, not respiting his Souldiers day or night, drew up all his Ships, and entrench'd them round within the circuit of his Camp. This don, and leaving to thir defence the same strength as before, he returns with his whole Forces to the same Wood, where he had defeated the *Britans*: who preventing him with greater powers then before, had now repossess'd themselvs of that place, under *Cassibelan* thir cheif Leader. Whose Territory from the States bordering on the Sea was divided by the *River Thames* about 80 mile inward. (V, 51-52)

Milton's summation lays bare the essence of the facts themselves. His historical narrative style offers maximum verbal economy and clarity, thereby duplicating the "plain, and lightsom brevity" he professed admiration for (V, 4). Short sentence members, a high percentage of elliptical constructions, frequent punctuation, and a noticeable dependence upon verbs add up to a rapid narrative flow. Authorial presence is negligible; it would be inappropriate in a context where Milton prefers to let the facts speak for themselves. Nor does he attempt to impose an hierarchical order upon those facts by presenting them in the periodic style. Instead, his linear, asymmetrical syntax sets before us a faceless procession of details, bits of data fit together with coordinating conjunctions, implying an almost random flow, rather than subordinated to connote pattern or interrelationship. Elliptical, curt, tonally neutral, barren of figurative language, his style mirrors the events it transcribes.

The style of historical narration differs from the oratorical low style of narration chiefly in its elliptical compression, in its preoccupation with facts, and in the reduced role it allows for an authorial persona; the historical style is not, in short, a "personal" style. In the letter to de Brass Milton voiced a preference for the style of Sallust, citing the ability of Sallust to "say much in a few words." That Sallust rejected the periodic sentence for historical writing has been established by Sir Ronald Syme.[65] Like Sallust's, Milton's narrative style is "abrupt"; it states facts "not in a hierarchy, but one by one, as they present themselves to the observer."[66] In addition, Wesley Trimpi has shown that Sallust was considered "as an early example of the Senecan stylistic virtues."[67] Milton's historical style is anything but periodic. Its elliptical terseness and avoidance of smooth syntactical transitions liken it to the disjunctive Senecanism practiced by many of his contemporaries.

II

Exacting though it may be, Milton's reconstruction of Britain's past is subordinate to his moral measurement of the nation's deeds. As noted earlier, the Christian historian considered history to be a storehouse of ethical exempla. Since the essence of oratory is to move the reader to action, the Christian historian's function is akin to that of the orator, for the historian approaches history from a moral point of view and attempts to persuade his audience to accept the conclusions he draws. History and oratory were, of course, closely allied in classical rhetorical theory; Cicero listed history as a division of epideictic oratory,[68] whose duty is praise and blame. When Milton turns from recording to evaluating deeds in the *History*, he assumes the rights and obligations of the epideictic orator. Above all, he gains the traditional oratorical freedom with facts. When the data at hand points to a moral meaning outside itself, the orator will alert the reader to that meaning, and, more importantly, he will presume to arrange facts to connote meaning. In effect, the Christian historian shares so many of the orator's prerogatives that he may be justly designated an orator.

Milton's oratorical mission in the *History* is to bring to light the pervasive moral paradigm he has discerned in British history: as a direct result of sacrificing their moral freedom, the Britons and Saxons were deprived of their political freedom. Having perceived this paradigm because of his heightened spiritual sensitivity,[69] the orator attempts to demonstrate the exact nature of the moral transgressions instrumental in the decline of two nations. His intrusions into the factual flow of narrative alert the reader to the moral meaning of historical data. Epideictic praise and blame, then, take on a special significance in the *History* as devices by which the orator discovers the hand of Providence in the affairs of men. Unlike his function as a collector of facts, which remains one-dimensional and constant throughout the tract, Milton's oratorical voice rises in pitch as the *History* progresses.

Not wishing to build his homily on "things wherof the substance is so much in doubt" (V, 37), Milton does not initiate his revelation of the Providential plan until he has finished reconstructing the legendary era of Britain's past. Freed by a "variety of good Authors" from the burdensome duty of separating fact from fantasy, Milton begins in earnest in Book III to subject the "unsound exploits" of the Britons to his "searching stile" (V, 40). His methodology is apparent in this evaluation of King Vortigern:

> But *Guortemir* now dead, and none of courage left to defend the Land, *Vortigern* . . . reassumes the Goverment: and *Hengist* thus rid of his grand opposer, hearing gladly the restorement of his old favourer, returns again with great Forces; *but to Vortigern whom he well knew how to handle without warring, as to his Son in Law*, now that the only Author of dissention between them was remov'd by Death, *offers nothing but all terms of new league and amity. The King both for his Wives sake and his own sottishness, consulting also with his Peers not unlike himself, readily yeilds;* and the place of parly is agree'd on; to which either side was to repair without Weapons. *Hengist*, whose meaning was not peace, but treachery, appointed his men to be secretly arm'd . . . when the *Britans* were throughly heated with Wine . . . [they were] dispatch'd . . . to the number of 300 . . . *Vortigern* they only bound and kept in Custody, untill he granted them for his ransome three Provinces. (V, 153-54; my italics in ll. 5-10)

Milton's sarcastic tone conveys his estimate of the reasons for Vortigern's fate. Rather than treating him as a helpless victim or the pawn of historical forces beyond his understanding, Milton suggests that Vortigern had control over his destiny: his weak will and self-indulgent nature betrayed him. Hence Vortigern was morally responsible, and therefore culpable, for the weakened condition in which he found himself. A moral coward is easy prey for political predators such as Hengist; indeed, moral weakness invites such predators. Milton's assessment of the Britons after their Roman protectors left sounds a similar note:

> For although at first greedy of change, and to be thought the leading Nation to freedom from the Empire, they seem'd a

> while to bestirr them with a shew of diligence in thir new
> affairs, som secretly aspiring to rule, others adoring the
> name of liberty, yet so soon as they felt by proof the weight
> of what it was to govern well themselves, and what was want-
> ing within them, not stomach or the love of licence, but the
> wisdom, the virtue, the labour, to use and maintain true
> libertie, they soon remitted thir heat, and shrunk more
> wretchedly under the burden of thir own libertie, than be-
> fore under a foren yoke. (V, 130-31)

His satirical indictment reveals that the Britons lacked the will
to defend themselves. Pampered, morally corrupt ("stomach . . .
love of licence"), devious ("some secretly aspiring to rule"), ob-
sessed with glittering exteriors ("the name of liberty"), they were
eager to cast off the burden of moral liberty and thus, appropriately, to insure their eventual political defeat and subjugation.
Again, Milton offers neither sociological nor economic rationaliza-
tions, laying the blame squarely on the faltering moral character
of the nation.

That Milton intended the aforementioned two evaluations to be
representative of the Britons as a people is indicated by his summary of the British decline in the closing lines of Book III:

> Thus omitting Fables, we have the veiw of what with reason
> can be rely'd on for truth, don in *Britain*, since the *Romans*
> forsook it. Wherin we have heard the many miseries and
> desolations, brought by divine hand on a perverse Nation;
> driv'n, when nothing else would reform them, out of a fair
> Country, into a Mountanous and Barren Corner, by Strang-
> ers and Pagans. So much more tolerable in the Eye of Heav'n
> is Infidelity profess't, then Christian Faith and Religion dis-
> honoured by unchristian works. (V, 183)

His appraisal emphatically asserts a Christian view of history.
The inexorable force of retributive justice, verifying the existence
of moral cause and effect in human affairs, meted out punishment
to a guilty nation; a morally unfit people could hardly expect to
escape political thralldom. In effect, the facts Milton has enumerated about the Britons ultimately point to an uncompromisingly
moral conclusion.

For the most part, the Saxons share with their British predecessors the same unfortunate assortment of debilitating vices. Milton
finds the Saxons uniquely blameworthy, however, in their persis-
tent efforts to purchase freedom monetarily from the pillaging
Danes, and he indicts them accordingly:

> [Ethelred] and his Courtiers wearied out with thir last
> Summers jaunt after the nimble *Danes* to no purpose, which
> by proof they found too toilsome for thir soft Bones, more
> us'd to Beds and Couches, had recourse to thir last and only
> remedy, thir Cofers; and send now the fourth time to buy
> a dishonorable peace, every time still dearer, not to be had
> now under 36 thousand pound (for the *Danes* knew how to
> milk such easie Kine) . . . which out of the people over all
> *England*, already half beggered, was extorted and paid. (V,
> 342)

Beneath Milton's sarcasm lies a contempt for the materialism of
the King and his followers, cowards guilty of both spinelessness
and extortion. Having played into the hands of predators delighted
to relieve them of their money, they turn predators themselves,
and steal from a populace already weakened and distressed. Their
self-indulgence and treachery, we are encouraged to conclude, led
naturally to such contemptible knavery. Ethelred and his followers are morally bankrupt. The inevitable consequence of their
attempt to fight with money instead of arms is to relinquish control of the state at periodic intervals to the marauding Danes. And
the Danes are no better than the weaklings who permitted them
to seize power, as is evident from Milton's discussion of Canute.
After defeating his Saxon opponents, Canute set out piously to
pacify his subjects, encouraged obedience to "the antient *Saxon*
Laws," and took up the guise of a saintly ruler (V, 358-65) by
freely owning up to his past sins. But Milton is not deceived: "But
it is a fond conceit in many great ones, and pernicious in the end,
to cease from no violence till they have attain'd the utmost of thir
ambitions and desires; then to think God appeas'd by thir seeking
to bribe him with a share however large of thir ill-gott'n spoils,
and then lastly to grow zealous of doing right, when they have no
longer need to do wrong" (V, 365). Like the Saxons, Canute is
guilty of bribery, but of an even more ignoble kind. His Machiavellian contempt for ethical standards in political matters betrays
a willingness to violate the moral order in order to erect a specious
political tranquility. His kingdom will be ill-fated, Milton implies,
and likely to fall before usurpers equally arrogant, but politically
stronger than he. Hypocrisy ("and pernicious in the end") begets
its own kind.

Milton's final indictment of the Saxons, although a paraphrase
of Malmesbury, recalls his earlier indictment of the Britons:

Not a few years before the Normans came, the Clergy,

> though in *Edward* the Confessors daies, had lost all good
> literature and Religion, scarse able to read and understand
> thir Latin Service . . . . The great men giv'n to
> gluttony and dissolute life, made a prey of the common
> people, abuseing thir Daughters whom they had in service,
> then turning them off to the Stews, the meaner sort tipling
> together night and day, spent all they had in Drunk'ness,
> attended with other Vices which effeminate mens minds.
> (V, 402)

He portrays a nation in decadence, one whose moral fibre has
disintegrated, making "easie" the Norman Conquest. "Some few"
upright men are left, but in the main both leaders and followers,
clergy and laymen have cast aside their moral liberty. The retributive justice of the Norman Conquest will be their lot.

The "searching stile" with which Milton surveys the "unsound
exploits" of the Britons and Saxons is in essence the low style of
satire adapted to the epideictic function of blame. The persuasiveness of his vehement rhetoric derives in part from the fixed moral
perspective which animates it; we are reminded that cowardly,
hypocritical conduct is blameworthy in any age because human
behavior is bonded together by immutable moral precepts. By appealing to our moral sensitivity, then, the orator convinces us
that the Britons and Saxons merited punishment for their evil
deeds. Milton's homiletic intention is to evoke in us through his
satiric tone and diction feelings of revulsion and dismay toward
the crimes he recounts, feelings clearly shared by the orator himself. The reader is moved to disavow the corruption he has witnessed by the pathetic and ethical proof at the core of Milton's
zealous didacticism, and not by detached, factual analyses of
economic or political processes.

Milton's treatment of the "unsound exploits" of the Britons and
Saxons in a common style underlines the moral axiom he considered applicable to both. In his view, the "propensity to sin"
leads to the "commission of sin" and ultimately to the "punishment of sin."[70] C. H. Firth has argued correctly that Milton
thought of each successive conquest of Britain as a "just judgement on the conquered race."[71] Milton's faith in the validity of
the sin-punishment axiom surely inspired his direct application
of it, in the Digression, to contemporary times. Positioning the
Digression at the beginning of Book III is pivotal, for Milton's
damning of the Long Parliament is equally effective in summariz-
ing his denunciation of the Britons, in anticipating his scorning of

the Saxons, and in glancing far ahead to the seventeenth century where it offers an evaluation of events past and a prophecy of those to come. The Long Parliament stands accused of the same crimes which precipitated the downfall of the Britons and Saxons. Its leaders are materialistic, greedy, self-serving, guilty of repeated betrayals of *"The Public Faith,"* and Milton can hardly conceal his doubts, as well, about the public's willingness to bear the burden of liberty. The thrust of his indictment is captured in this passage:

> [Parliamentarians] and to be sure the greatest part whom wealth and ample possessions or bold and active ambition rather then merit had commended to the same place, when onc[e] the superficial zeale and popular fumes that acted thir new magistracie were cool'd and spent in them, straite every one betooke himself, setting the common-wealth behinde and his private ends before, to doe as his owne profit or ambition led him . . . . And if the *State* were in this plight, *Religion* was not in much better . . . . Yet these Conscientious [Divines] . . . wanted not boldness, to the Ignominy and Scandal of their Pastor-like Profession, and especially of their boasted Reformation, to seize into their hands, or not unwillingly to accept . . . Collegiate Masterships in the Universities, rich Lectures in the City, setting Sail to all Winds that might blow Gain into their covetous Bosoms. (V, 443-46)

The satirist's irate tone and slashing diction focus on the odious discrepancy between the promises of Parliamentarians and their performance, between the ideals of clerics and the "Ignominy and Scandal" they are party to, between a nation's commitment to Reformation and its moral laxity. The periodic syntax of the passage itself connotes cause and effect, the continuity of past, present, and future time: England in the 1640's staggers ever closer to the moral quagmire which swallowed the Britons and Saxons. Milton's voice is both persuasive and prophetic. Reformation will surely be stillborn unless a return to moral rectitude occurs. Instead of achieving political and moral liberty, England will find itself again enslaved to episcopacy and monarchy. The orator declares the will of Providence.[72]

Milton's effort in the Digression to strike a parallel between past and present time foreshadows the oratorical freedom with facts which he will exercise with increasing frequency in subsequent books of the *History*. In effect, Milton progresses from com-

menting on deeds he deems morally relevant to arranging the
facts at his command to demonstrate the hand of Providence at
work. Existing side by side with satirical indictments which emphasize blame and the moral turmoil stirred up by evildoers,
Milton's exemplary incidents connote harmony and clarify the
ideals implicit in his condemnation of the Britons and Saxons. One
such incident is drawn from the life of the Saxon King Edmund.
Milton's sketch of Edmund's reign is brief, most of his facts being
selected from the *Anglo-Saxon Chronicle*, facts which add up to a
portrait of a warlike and treacherous leader, not inclined to abide
by contractual or ethical promises (V, 315-16). Edmund's cruelty
shows itself in his blinding of the two sons of *"Dummail* the
Cumbrian King," after depriving their father of his kingdom.
Having reviewed these events, Milton pauses to linger over one
day in Edmund's life:

> [Edmund] feasting with his Nobles on St. *Austins* Day at
> *Puclekerke* in *Glostershire*, to celebrat the memory of his
> first converting the *Saxons*. He spi'd *Leof* a noted Theef,
> whom he had banish'd, sitting among his Guests; wherat
> transported with too much vehemence of Spirit, though in
> a just cause, riseing from the Table he ran upon the Theef,
> and catching his hair, pull'd him to the ground. The Theef
> who doubted from such handling no less then his Death in-
> tended, thought to die not unreveng'd; and with a short Dag-
> ger strook the King . . . mortally into the brest. (V, 317)

The episode, which takes up nearly half of the space devoted to
Edmund's reign, is reconstructed from several sources, for the
Chronicle notes only the date of the King's death.[73] Milton's
considered arrangement of details encourages the reader, already
alerted to the moral value of mankind's deeds by Milton's satiric
interjections, to view the event as exemplary, the facts as symbols
of a non-factual reality. That reality is the recurring Providential
intervention into human affairs. Appropriately, a cruel and thievish
king, who had recently stolen a kingdom, is removed suddenly and
violently by a thief. After reading of endless disruptions of the
moral universe by the Britons and Saxons, the reader might take
heart in the assertion of Providential power in the form of a
greedy, malicious ruler's punishment. Symbolically, the incident
embodies the harmony of moral cause and effect.

Milton's treatment of King Alfred exhibits the same oratorical
freedom with fact, fulfilling the epideictic function of praise but
in a more explicit fashion than did the episode of Leof and Ed-

mund. He delineates Alfred as a "miror of Princes," the antithesis of his ignoble contemporaries. He builds from Asser, Malmesbury, and the *Chronicle* the composite and exemplary portraiture
of a man distinguished by the "glorious labours of his life both
in peace and war" (V, 292). If the facts of Alfred's reign seem to
weaken the positive impression Milton wishes to leave, he intervenes in Alfred's behalf. Milton excuses Alfred's apparent failure
to check completely the Danish depredations by observing: "the
French and *Flemish* were no more able then the *English*, by Policy
or prowess to keep off that *Danish* inundation from thir land"
(V, 281). He omits, moreover, a report in the *Chronicle* of "Pope
Martin's sending a piece of the True Cross to Alfred,"[74] thereby
freeing Alfred from the charges of popish superstition and sub-
servience to Rome which he had leveled at other Saxon rulers.
Milton attributes to the king's youthfulness ("through jollity of
mind unwilling perhaps to be detain'd long with sad and sorrowful
Narrations") his occasional failure to heed the "complaints of such
as injur'd and oppress'd repair'd to him . . . for redress" (V, 290).

The nobility of Alfred deserves the immortality afforded by
eloquence, and Milton enhances the reader's opinion of Alfred
with eulogies such as the following:

> But from the time of his undertaking regal charge, no man
> more patient in hearing causes, more inquisitive in examin-
> ing, more exact in doing justice, and providing good Laws,
> which are yet extant; more severe in punishing unjust judges
> or obstinate offenders. Theeves especially and Robbers, to
> the terrour of whom in cross waies were hung upon a high
> Post certain Chains of Gold, as it were dareing any one to
> take them thence; so that justice seem'd in his daies not to
> flourish only, but to tryumph. (V, 290-91)

To celebrate the deeds of Alfred Milton selects the oratorical
middle style, lending grace and smoothness to his eulogy through
anaphora ("more patient . . . more severe"), *isocolon*, and *parison*.
In Alfred Milton finds the ideal combination of action and con-
templation: Alfred is concerned with the political safety of his
countrymen, but more importantly, with their intellectual and
moral well-being. Unlike his Saxon predecessors and his descend-
ants in the seventeenth century, Alfred's precepts are wed to his
practices. If Milton's attacks on Briton and Saxon excesses were
intended to have contemporary relevance, so also is his praise of
Alfred. Led by statesmen of this kind, a Christian Commonwealth
could flourish in accordance with Providential design.

III

By pointing out the moral flaws which brought the Britons and Saxons to ruin and by eulogizing the virtues which allowed Alfred to escape such an end, Milton expected to foster a national recognition of the ever-present need for moral rectitude on the part of both leaders and followers. His homily implies a firm hope that the cycle of sin and punishment evident in British history can be checked. If the orator's zealous homily is heeded, Reformation might yet be realized. However, in Books V and VI, those composed during the 1650's,[75] Milton sounds his awareness of yet another pattern in the events he narrates, one more comprehensive and ominous than the specific events of British history he records. The pattern has been described succinctly by French Fogle: "Within human time, at least, there was no general advance toward a discernible goal, no wave-like movement toward the redeemed society. Only the continuing malignancy of pride and passions in senseless conflict, until the final decisive act of judgment should destroy time and history with it."[76] Competing with his homiletic thrusts in the final books, particularly in Book VI, is Milton's reluctant realization that British history, far from being the edifying record of God's elect nation, is but a minute, unsavory chapter of postlapsarian human history, and is, therefore, a disheartening legacy of strife and regression. What Milton had begun to perceive in Britain's past would have been reenforced by his personal experience of a Holy Commonwealth torn by "pride and passions in senseless conflict." One may discern Milton's growing enervation in the stance he takes toward several events related in the closing books, a stance which points up the pervasiveness of postlapsarian weakness and unregeneracy. Milton's posture is revealed by his treatment of the Machiavellian scheming of King Harold, who, after apparently seizing the throne,[77]

> began to frame himself by all manner of compliances to gain affection, endeavour'd to make good Laws, repeal'd bad, became a great Patron to Church and Churchmen, courteous and affable to all reputed good, a hater of evill doers, charg'd all his Officers to punish Theeves, Robbers, and all disturbers of the peace, while he himself by Sea and Land labour'd in the defence of his Country: *so good an actor is ambition.*
> (V, 394; my italics)

Milton's climactic remark is curt, factual, devoid of the angry tone and zealous denunciation integral to his polemic mode. His stance connotes a weary acceptance of the profound discrepancies between appearance and reality in political matters, the sad lot of the postlapsarian world. Vanity, treachery, pretension, he implies, are irremediable; hence he refuses to launch a polemic tirade, but rests content with stating this truth as he perceives it.

He treats another episode similarly:

> [*Elmer* a *Monk* of *Malmsbury*] in his youth strangely aspiring, had made and fitted Wings to his Hands and Feet; with these on the top of a Tower, spread out to gather air, he flew more then a Furlong; but the wind being too high, came fluttering down, to the maiming of all his Limbs; yet so conceited of his Art, that he attributed the cause of his fall to the want of a Tail, as Birds have, which he forgot to make to his hinder parts. (V, 394-95)

Clearly the anecdote is of no immediate factual value; on the contrary, it seems to be an unwarranted intrusion into the sketch of events just prior to the Norman Conquest which Milton had been constructing. Yet its metaphoric overtones are broadly suggestive, as were those of the earlier tale about Harold. Again, an ironic tone predominates, one which approaches comedy. In the monk's plight we may witness, in microcosm, the perennial blindness, the lack of insight into even the simplest matters, the penchant for making a fool of oneself which plagues the postlapsarian world. Indeed, as Milton observes, the story is "light," for it captures the often comic inadequacies of mankind's lot after the Fall. Milton's objectivity and detachment magnify the irony in his story: man reduces himself to the absurd by his failure to perceive the divergence of truth and falsehood. The same detached tone dominates his final prophetic overview of Britain's past: "If these were the Causes of such misery and thraldom to those our Ancestors, with what better close can be concluded, then here in fit season to remember this Age in the midst of her security, to fear from like Vices without amendment the Revolutions of like Calamities" (V, 403). In sharp contrast to the fiery prophecy of the Digression, Milton's epilogue is a tacit recognition that the prophet can predict but not persuade. Milton had witnessed in the withering away of the Commonwealth the culmination of a cycle of sin and retribution he had feared, and perhaps anticipated, in the 1640's. Perceiving the futility of attempting to convince a heedless nation, Milton records for posterity a profound truth likely to recur throughout human history. He does so with the conviction that even if no one hears the prophet's message, he is nevertheless justified in proclaiming it, for his is the voice of Providence.

The effects of the *History of Britain* are varied. In his role as historian Milton rescued a considerable part of Britain's past from the limbo of factual omissions, inaccuracies, and mythological distortions. Simultaneously, he brought to light a moral paradigm which he expounded upon in his role as epideictic orator. Milton's moral reading of British history makes plain not only the reasons for his ancestors' slide into slavery, but, by analogy, the reasons why the Commonwealth dissolved and Reformation on a national level was thwarted. Although there is much to disdain in Britain's past, Milton also shapes, on both a public and a personal level, several redemptive patterns. King Alfred, the mirror of princes, whose reign was blessed by Providence, is an exemplum of regenerate political conduct. If Reformation were to succeed in time future, leaders of Alfred's caliber would be necessary. Yet, particularly in the final books, Milton ministered to the needs of the individual regenerate reader, who, in all times and places, would discover the root causes for Britain's recurrent decline. More important, the regenerate reader would detect in the reactions and evaluations of the narrator a paradigm of regenerate behavior worthy of imitation. In his zealous moral appraisals of denunciation and eulogy, Milton manifests the regenerate spiritual sensitivity, the ability to pierce through the factual surface of events to their inner moral significance, which is the essence of Christian freedom. In particular, his awareness and celebration of King Alfred's integrity mark him as one whose own moral qualities are no less distinguished; he who would eulogize "worthy deeds" must experience them himself. Although the reader may grow weary of an unregenerate world of corrupt institutions and faltering leaders, he will find sustenance in the knowledge that to exercise his Christian freedom as the narrator did is to experience the "paradise within."

Milton Disputing

It has been recognized that the "conventions of seventeenth-century controversy permitted either the dignified decorum of sober defense or the undignified display of a kind of pen-lashing."[78] As surely as Milton indulged in "pen-lashing," he met the demands of scholarly debate. *Of Prelatical Episcopacy* and *Tetrachordon*, without parallel in the Milton canon for the breadth of their erudition,[79] are specimens of rigorous argument in which Aristotelian logic and metaphysics, church histories, and exegetical commentaries are summoned to support Milton's doctrinal positions. In each tract Milton had recourse to the Renaissance art of disputation. After a preliminary sketch of the conventions of disputation in the seventeenth century, I shall turn to the Fourth and Fifth *Prolusions* where Milton first utilized those conventions. In *Prelatical Episcopacy* and *Tetrachordon* Milton transformed the mode of academic debate practiced in his Cambridge days into a rhetorical device capable of moving learned churchmen and intelligent, if unlearned, laymen alike. His dialectic invariably resolves the issues under debate into irreconcilable antitheses, thereby simplifying the reader's choice of alternatives. I will demonstrate, finally, that Milton's public-to-personal rhetorical paradigm allowed him considerable flexibility and persuasiveness as a disputant.

Traceable perhaps to the scholastic disputations of the medieval universities, the art of disputation survived as part of the academic curriculum well into the seventeenth century. Along with the lecture and the declamation, the disputation was one of the principal academic exercises at Cambridge during Milton's undergraduate career.[80] Disputations both public and private on a wide range of subjects were fundamental to the student's training and demanded that he familiarize himself with the "works of Aristotle, particularly the *Organon*, the ethics, the *Rhetoric*, and the metaphysics."[81] Disputants, in search of a precise formulation of truths bearing on the question at issue, found the intricate syllogistic format of Aristotelian logic necessary to achieve their objective. According to the rules of Aristotelian dialectic, a disputation called for a critical examination of the premises and consequences of an opponent's thesis, as well as an attempt to render one's own case logically consistent and comprehensive. The disputative method prompted a constant exchange of affirmative and negative arguments between the two contestants, each relying on the strategy of "interrogation and response" and directing a variety of syllogisms at his opponent in order to force a particular point from him.[82]

The methodology of disputation was treated exhaustively in many of the textbooks of logic used by Cambridge students. A concise summary of the accepted conventions can be found in Abraham Fraunce's *The Lawiers Logike* and Thomas Wilson's *The Rule of Reason*.[83] Since both manuals were part of the extensive reading in logic required of any student before he engaged in disputation, Milton's familiarity with them seems beyond doubt. Wilson's definition of the conduct of the disputation fits the sort of logical exercise Milton was to perform in the *Prolusions*: "either we purpose by disputation, to aunswere fully to the matter, or els secondly (if power want to compasse that) we seeke some other meanes, to satisfie the man, and that three maner of waies, either by making the objection seem lesse then it is, or by bringing some other example against it, or els by seeking some meanes, to goe from the matter."[84]

In effect, Wilson contends that a disputation may be conducted by either logical, or non-logical means (i.e., by using the Aristotelian categories of pathetic, ethical, or artificial proof).[85] Fraunce sets forth the "direct solution" to a debate question:

1) By denying either of
   a) The premisses and prosyllogisms when they be false
   b) Or the consecution & consequence, when the fault is in the forme of conclusion: for the conclusion it selfe must never be denied.

2) By distinguishing when either
   a) The questions and interrogations be captious and doubtfull,
   b) Or the premisses bee true not absolutely, but in part . . .
   c) Or conditionall graunting, as I graunt, if you so understand it.

3) . . . By bringing in some instance, that is by taking a particular exception to a general proposition.[86]

Both affirmative argument and refutation usually assumed the form of the syllogism, or its rhetorical equivalent, the enthymeme.

If a disputant were unable to "dissolve the argument, by the rules of Logicke," several other devices were available to him. As Wilson observes, one may make the opponent's "argument appear slender, when we receive it laughingly, and declare by wordes, even at the first, that is nothying to the purpose, and so abash the opponent" (63ᵛ). One could belittle an opponent's argument by using several related rhetorical devices, including: *Apodioxis* (rejecting a thesis as "needlesse, absurde [or] false"); *Metastasis* (turning back "those thinges that are objected against us to them which laid them to us"); and *Antirrhesis* (denying the "authority, opinion or sentence of some person: for the error or wickednesse of it").[87] Scoffing at an opponent's plea, is, of course, a way of eliciting pathetic proof against it. The same objective is achieved when "wee shift away from the violence of our adversarie, by making some digression, or giving occasion of some other talke, whereby the adversarie, either is driven to forget his argument, or els being blinded with too much matter, is forced either to goe no further, or els to thinke himselfe content" (63ᵛ). Digression might involve not only pathetic and ethical proof, but also a heightened style of affective diction and imagery. Wilson calls as well for the judicious use of examples in a disputation, in the following manner:

1) By using the same example [that an opponent used] in an other matter . . .
2) By makyng a cleane contrary example . . . . (82ʳ⁻ᵛ)

Finally, the disputant could avail himself of artificial proof "By standing to authoritie, or using sentences of the sage" (82ʳ⁻ᵛ).

The conventions of disputation summarized above are exemplified in Milton's Fourth and Fifth *Prolusions*. Both tracts explore philosophical dilemmas arising from Aristotelian metaphysics, and both rely upon logical dialectic to resolve them, to separate true from false in the question at issue. Each is structured in the manner of the medieval disputation, notably those of Thomas Aquinas:

1) Rhetorical introduction.
2) Statement of the question to be argued.
3) General account of the *sententiae* or opinions of previous philosophers for and against the thesis.
4) Defendant's own logical proofs based upon arguments taken from the *sententiae* affirming the thesis.
5) Defendant's answers to the unfavorable *sententiae*.[88]

Prolusion Four, "In the Destruction of any Substance there can be no Resolution into First Matter," illustrates the complex dialectical interplay which bears the burden of proof in each disputation. In the following instance, Milton advances and then qualifies one of the central arguments of his thesis:

> Secondly, if an accident is destroyed, it can only be destroyed in one of the following ways — either by the introduction of a contrary, or by cessation of its term, or by the absence of some other conserving cause, or, lastly, by the defect of the proper subject in which it inheres. Quantity cannot be destroyed in the first way, since it has no contrary; and although quality has, this must not be substituted here: the second way does not apply, since it is proper to relatives; nor by the absence of a conserving cause, for that which my opponents assign is form. (I, 252-53)

Through logical deduction Milton discards as irrelevant two of the stated ways in which an accident may be destroyed. On other occasions, he strikes precise logical distinctions in order to rebut the postulates of his opponents. Here he concedes one point but forces them to grant another: "Thirdly, Aristotle says that when primary substances are destroyed all accidents are destroyed. We do not deny that this will happen, provided you grant that another may immediately succeed that which was destroyed" (I, 254).

In *Prolusion Five*, "There are no partial Forms in an Animal in addition to the Whole," Milton calls up the authority of the Dominican scholar Chrysostom Javello to buttress his case.[89] Javello's pronouncements to the effect that "The distinction and organisation of dissimilar parts" of the body "must precede the introduction of the soul" into the body are first presented in detail, and then the conclusions necessary to Milton's subsequent argument are extracted from them. The interaction of logic and authority in *Prolusion Five* is indicative of Milton's skill in bringing two distinct modes of proof to bear simultaneously upon the point at issue. The predominantly logical appeal of both *Prolusions* necessitates his reliance upon a plain style which focuses the reader's attention upon the systematic explication taking place.

II

With the skill of a seasoned polemicist cognizant of an "audience" considerably more heterogeneous than collegiate "sophisters," Milton forged, in *Prelatical Episcopacy* and *Tetrachordon*, the weapons of disputation he had tested in the *Prolusions* into a potent rhetorical implement. In both tracts Milton sought not only to satisfy the demands of scholarly readers, but also to elicit a response from a larger audience composed primarily of intellectually unsophisticated Christians whose limited education would prevent them from comprehending fully or evaluating erudite dialectic.[90] In effect, Milton hoped to translate the complex matters he debated into universally intelligible terms so that every reader could perceive the relationship of these issues to the Reformation. Consequently, Milton's mode of discourse is dualistic: his argument proceeds from particularized, technical disputation to evocation of emotional, subjective responses toward the question at hand. This procedure allows him to exploit a variety of proofs to win assent to his proposition.

In its dual character Milton's disputative style is like that of Jeremy Taylor. As Frank L. Huntley has observed, the argument of Taylor's Civil-War episcopal tracts splits into "two great halves."[91] *Of the Sacred Order and Offices of Episcopacy*, for example, examines episcopacy from two distinct perspectives, episcopacy "in itself" and episcopacy "for us."[92] As the argument progresses from "in itself" to "for us," Taylor's style evolves from "stern and factual" to "flowing" and "homely," while his method of proof shifts from logic and scholarly citation to "custom," "common sense," and "manners," which the "commonest man can understand and appreciate."[93] Although Taylor's dualism resembles Milton's, his resolution of the dichotomy asserted by his dialectic is quite the opposite. For the Anglican Taylor, episcopacy "in itself" and "for us" are finally synthesized into a totality representative of a more comprehensive truth, as befits the *via media*. Both Milton and Taylor juxtapose such values as tradition and Scripture. But Milton's Puritan dialectic posits a hierarchy in which one value (Scripture) clearly transcends the other (tradition). Each term aids in defining the other, yet they remain distinct, having been hurled into antithetical opposition by the force of Milton's polemic.

In *Prelatical Episcopacy* Milton challenges the erudite contentions of the Anglican apologists Bishop Joseph Hall, Archbishop James Ussher, and the pseudonymous Peloni Almoni Cosmopolites. Hall's *Episcopacie by Divine Right Asserted*, Ussher's *The Judgement of Doctor Rainoldes*, and Almoni's *A Compendious Discourse*, all of which were issued in 1640-1641,[94] clarify in exhaustive detail the theological rationale of episcopacy. Each apologist provides substantive scholarly citation, particularly from the

Church Fathers, as evidence for the divine sanctioning of the authority of bishops and archbishops. Almoni stresses the testimony of Irenaeus and Polycarp, and Ussher the writings of Ignatius. Hall's *Episcopacie* assembles a more extensive and varied list of citations to the same effect, and repeatedly draws the logical conclusion that episcopal rule finds its sanction in Christian tradition. The Anglican tracts share a scholarly tone, a dignified presentation of testimony and logical argument, and a definite if unintended restriction to a learned public presumably composed of churchmen.

Prelatical Episcopacy challenges the fundamental premises of the episcopal position and simultaneously validates the consistency of the Puritan counter-assertion that Scripture ordains church government by presbyters alone. Milton's critical examination of the consequences of both Anglican and Puritan positions demanded the methodology of the dialectical disputation. Hence his argument focuses upon logical probability in determining the likelihood of the accuracy of each claim. The effect of the disputative method is to separate the truth of the Bible from the error of tradition.

The structure of *Prelatical Episcopacy* resembles that of *Prolusions Four* and *Five*. Its rhetorical introduction and conclusion, roughly analogous to the exordium and peroration of an oration, are exceptionally brief, serving only to define the subject of debate ("Epyscopacy . . . is either of Divine constitution, or of humane"), and to announce that all of the arguments have been presented. Structural emphasis in *Prelatical Episcopacy* is given, as it was in the *Prolusions*, to a lengthy, involved dialectic which summarizes the conclusions of the episcopal tracts and proposes to answer all three simultaneously. In the following example, Milton questions an authority (*Leontius Bishop* of *Magnesia*) cited by Ussher "to prove a succession of 27. *Bishops* from *Timothy*" (I, 627). Milton's erudition is evident in his reference to another Church Father who dealt with the question of succession:

> Much rather should we attend to what *Eusebius* the ancientest writer extant of Church-history . . . confesses in the 4. chap. of his 3. Book, that it was no easie matter to tell who were those that were left Bishops of the Churches by the Apostles, more then by what a man might gather from the *Acts* of the Apostles, and the Epistles of St. *Paul*, in which number he reckons *Timothy* for Bishop of *Ephesus*. (I, 630-31)

The testimony of Eusebius constitutes an inductive proof which undermines the validity of the inference Ussher drew from Leontius. Having established an inductive theorem, Milton proceeds to extract its logical consequences, based upon the argument from probability: "Now if *Eusebius* a famous writer thought it so difficult to tell who were appointed Bishops by the Apostles, much more may we think it difficult to *Leontius* an obscure Bishop speaking beyond his own Diocesse" (I, 631). He then posits a further deductive consequence, one which strikes at the essence of the Anglican argument from tradition: "and much lesse reason have we to stand to [the Fathers'] definitive sentence, seeing they have bin so rash to raise up such lofty Bishops and Bishopricks out of places in Scripture meerly misunderstood" (I, 631).

The combination of scholarly authority and logical analysis evident above is repeated in Milton's numerous specific objections to the ponderous structure of the episcopal position. Thus he denies a major premise of his opponents:

> Next follows *Irenaeus* Bishop of *Lions*, who is cited to affirm *that Polycarpus was made Bishop of Smyrna by the Apostles* . . . . It will not be deny'd that [Irenaeus] might have seen *Polycarpus* in his youth a man of great eminence in the Church, to whom the other *Presbyters* might give way for his *vertue, wisdome*, and the reverence of his age . . . . but that we should hence conclude a distinct, and superior order from the young observation of *Irenaeus*, nothing yet alledg'd can warrant us. (I, 639-40)

The "observation" of a youth is not a firm basis for belief, another version of the argument from probability. Here Milton grants a point, but disallows, in Wilson's words, the "consecution and consequence" of the major and minor premises in the resulting episcopal syllogism: "We grant them Bishops, we grant them worthy men, we grant them plac't in severall Churches by the *Apostles*, we grant that *Irenaeus*, and *Tertul*: affirme this, but that they were plac't in a superior Order above the *Presbytery*, shew from all these words why we should grant" (I, 644-45). The following "concession" is an example of the rhetorical figure *Paromologia*, whereby a disputant grants something to his adversary that is "unfavorable to his own position, and then suddenly brings in a point which overthrows all that was granted."[95] Hence Milton concedes: "He that thinks it the part of a well learned man, to have read diligently the ancient stories of the Church, and to be no stranger in the volumes of the Fathers shall have all judicious men consenting with him" (I, 650). Yet one should "read diligently" not to find a rationale for episcopacy, but rather "to marke how corruption, and *Apostacy* crept in by degrees" (I, 650), a succinct negation of the entire episcopal position.

Although logical argument predominates in *Prelatical Episcopacy*, Milton employs several other devices of disputation mentioned by Wilson and Fraunce. One of these is example, something he had seldom used in the *Prolusions*. For the most part, Milton's examples are fully incorporated into his dialectical framework and act to buttress his major premises. In attacking the testimony of Ignatius, Milton relates several doctrinal points in the Ignatian Epistles which might be considered heretical, for instance: "In the Epistle to those of *Tarsus* he condemns them for Ministers of Satan, that say *Christ is God above all*" (I, 636).[96] This erratic bit of Ignatian wisdom becomes a rebuke to the Anglicans who extol the sanctity of Ignatian precepts. The example in question is a specimen of the "clean contrary example" discussed by Wilson. Wilson also advised that a disputant turn an opponent's example against him, and Milton does so: "As for those *Brittaine* Bishops which you cite, take heed what you doe, for our *Brittaine* Bishops lesse ancient then these, were remarkable for nothing more then their poverty, as *Sulp. Severus*, and *Beda* can remember you of examples good store" (I, 646-47). Not only do the *"Brittaine* Bishops" cited by the Anglicans fail to convince, but they call to mind the failings of modern bishops.

Following Wilson, Milton draws upon artificial proof as an antidote to the learned citations of the Anglicans. As were his examples, Milton's "testimony" is usually incorporated into a broader pattern of proof essentially logical in nature. His repeated references to Eusebius, "the ancientest writer extant of Church-history," are ample evidence to rebut the claims of Irenaeus and Polycarp and a vital link in the chain of inductive reasoning which exposes errors in the writings of other Church Fathers. Milton's most frequently quoted and indisputable source of authority is Scripture, which he constantly wields against the "traditions" of episcopacy. Scripture, Milton insists, is the "onely Book left us of *Divine* authority" and hence the only stable reference point in a tempest of conflicting data.

Logical analysis, example, and authority, then, constitute the main thrust of Milton's rebuttal of Anglican claims for the sanctity of episcopacy. Milton maintains a dignified, academic tone while repeatedly urging the reader to pursue the logical consequences of his affirmative and negative premises. As it was in the *Prolusions*,

Milton's argument is conducted in a plain, literal style virtually devoid of affective diction and imagery. In the following instance and elsewhere in the tract, Milton's purpose is to assemble facts and to establish their significance:

> [Tertullian] saies that the Church of *Smirna* had *Polycarpus* plac't there by *Iohn*, and the Church of *Rome Clement* ordain'd by *Peter*, and so the rest of the Churches did shew, what Bishops they had receiv'd by the appointment of the *Apostles*. None of this will be contradicted, for we have it out of the Scripture that Bishops or *Presbyters*, which were the same, were left by the *Apostles* in every Church, and they might perhaps give some speciall charge to *Clement*, or *Polycarpus*, or *Linus*, and put some speciall trust in them for the experience they had of their faith, and constancy; it remaines yet to be evinc't out of this and the like places, which will never be, that the word Bishop is otherwise taken, then in the language of Saint *Paul*, and the *Acts*, for an order above *Presbyters*. (I, 644)

The unembroidered diction and direct syntax of the passage call for the reader to make an objective evaluation and thereby to agree that Anglican "testimony" is inconclusive.

The effect of Milton's scholarly dialectic, which comprises more than sixty percent of his text, is to define the episcopal position as illogical, inconsistent, contradictory. The remainder of the tract reiterates in more widely intelligible terms the implications of that thesis. In translating his contention into universal terms, Milton relies heavily upon evocation, upon pathetic and ethical proof, instead of logical precision.[97] Yet his methodology remains within the context of debate in that his evocative devices are either those he had employed earlier and now turns to a different purpose, or recognized devices of disputation which he had not used previously. Here Milton offers an example which illustrates his premise that contradictions are inherent in the episcopal position:

> Tradition hath had very seldome or never the gift of perswasion; as that which Church Histories report of those *East*, and *Western Paschalists* formerly spoken of will declare, who would have thought that *Polycarpus* on the one side could have err'd in what he saw Saint *Iohn* doe, or *Anicetus* Bishop of *Rome* on the other side, in what he or some of his friends might pretend to have seene Saint *Peter*, or Saint *Paul* doe, and yet neither of these could perswade either when to keepe Easter; The like frivolous contention troubled

> the Primitive English Churches, while *Colmanus*, and *Wilfride* on either side deducing their opinions, the one from the undeniable example of Saint *Iohn*, and the learned Bishop *Anatolius*, and lastly the miraculous *Columba*: the other from Saint *Peter*. (I, 648)

Ironically, traditionalists themselves were often unable to agree upon the meaning of tradition. The implications of this example serve as a pathetic proof manifest to every reader: one ought to fear traditionalists. Their dissension bodes ill for the conduct of church government, and the enervating confusion they spawn lies in wait for all.

A Miltonic digression[98] concerning the rise of tradition after the death of the Apostles sounds a similar note:

> Where ever a man, who had bin any way conversant with the *Apostles*, was to be found, thether flew all the inquisitive eares, the exercise of right instructing was chang'd into the curiosity of impertinent fabling: where the mind was to be edified with solid *Doctrine*, there the fancy was sooth'd with solemne stories: with lesse fervency was studied what Saint *Paul*, or Saint *Iohn* had written then was listen'd to one that could say here hee taught, here he stood, this was his stature, and thus he went habited. (I, 641-42)

Tradition is no more than a record of human folly, a testament to the errors of fallen man who cannot distinguish between a glamorous falsehood and saving truth. In a cacophony of babbling and contradictory tongues, the message of the Gospel is lost. Milton's graphic illustration, a type of *reductio ad absurdum*, suggests to even the humblest reader that the hearsay and exaggeration of tradition ought to be greeted with skepticism. The tone of Milton's censure intensifies in his presentation of a story told about Polycarp:

> If *Polycarpus* (who, as they say, was a *Prophet* that never faild in what he foretold) had declar'd to his friends, that he knew by vision, hee should die no other death then burning, how it came to passe that the fire when it came to proofe, would not doe his worke, but starting off like a full saile from the mast, did but reflect a golden light upon his unviolated limbes exhaling such a sweet odour, as if all the incense of *Arabia* had bin burning, in so much that when the bill-men saw that the fire was overaw'd, and could not doe the deed, one of them steps to him, and stabs him with a sword, at

which wound such abundance of bloud gusht forth as quencht the fire. By all this relation it appeares not, how the fire was guilty of his death, and then how can his prophesie bee ful-fill'd? Next how the standers by could be so soone weary of such a glorious sight, and such a fragrant smell, as to hasten the executioner to put out the fire with the Martyrs blood, unlesse perhaps they thought, as in all perfumes, that the Smoake would bee more odorous then the flame? (I, 643)

While the tale has early authority, Milton's mocking sarcasm transforms it into a perfect specimen of the rhetorical figure *Apodioxis*, and a dramatic proof of his charge that tradition fre-quently makes sacrosanct the ludicrous, the irrational, and the unverifiable. In the case of Polycarp, naiveté, rumor, and imagina-tion prevail so that whatever significance the incident may have held — if, in fact, such an incident took place — has been gro-tesquely, comically distorted. And such "tradition" is the foun-dation of the episcopal position. Milton's mimicry, his ironic posture of earnest inquiry discredits the legend of Polycarp to the extent that the reader can readily assent to the ridicule and dis-missal of this sort of folly and those who uphold it.

Milton's strongest evocative pleas occur at the conclusion of *Prelatical Episcopacy*, the most effective moment rhetorically. In appealing to the deeply rooted Protestant hatred of Rome, Milton warns that following tradition threatens the very foundations of Reformation: "wee both forsake our owne grounds, and reasons which led us at first to part from *Rome*, that is to hold to the Scriptures against all antiquity; wee remove our cause into our adversaries owne Court, and take up there those cast principles which will soone cause us to soder up with them againe, in as much as beleeving antiquity for it self in any one point, we bring an ingagement upon our selves of assenting to all that it charges upon us" (I, 650).

The evocative arguments of *Prelatical Episcopacy* are displayed in a heightened style which blends a scornful, ironic tone with satiric imagery and caustic diction to compel the agreement of the common reader. Milton's imagistic attack on the romantic embellishment which reduces much of written tradition to the ab-surd — "that pavement bedew'd with the warme effusion of [one of the Apostles'] last blood, that sprouted up into eternall Roses to crowne his Martyrdome" (I, 642) — and his polemic denuncia-tion of the "inquisitive eares" which hearken to the superficial and neglect the truth win emotional assent to his position. The

evocative style elicits as well a broad response to Milton's affirmative argument. Instead of providing a detailed exegesis, Milton
repeatedly eulogizes the sanctity of Scripture, suggesting that his
readers examine it for themselves according to their individual
capacities and adhere to it in the spirit of humble faith and obedience. Consultation of Scripture will protect zealous Christians,
for Scripture gives the lie to the idle superstition which traditionalists confuse with truth. Its stability bolsters the faith of the
true believer and pierces the darkness of the dissension spread by
endless, futile debate over the precise meaning of tradition.

The dialectical curve of *Prelatical Episcopacy* has been from
scholarship to polemic. As the tract progresses, Milton's arguments evolve from complex and erudite to one-dimensional and
deliberately unsophisticated. Having opened with a careful analysis of episcopal sources (I, 624-39), Milton proceeds to emphasize
the inconsistency of the episcopal position (I, 639-48); to claim
that history bears witness to the confusion spawned by tradition
(I, 648-50); that Popery threatens to ensnare the traditionalist
(I, 650-51); and, finally, that questioning the sanctity of Scripture (I, 651-52) is little short of blasphemy. In the initial argument of the pamphlet logic and authority are omnipresent, but
non-logical, evocative pleas, which culminate in the incantation-
like final argument, eventually predominate. Milton's scholarly
objectivity gradually gives way to sarcasm, innuendo, and invective, his public, dignified tone to passionate personal intensity, and
his plain style to a comparatively ornate one. In effect, the detached, analytical stance evident at the outset of *Prelatical Episcopacy* yields to an intensely subjective, imaginative, at times
visionary conception of the episcopal controversy, and that conception finds its most appropriate articulation in indignant, zealous
polemic; the disputant himself becomes an emblem of the response
he wishes to evoke in the reader.

As I have demonstrated, Milton's dialectic is one of separation,
of polarization. In the latter arguments of *Prelatical Episcopacy*
the weapons of disputation listed in the manuals of Fraunce and
Wilson are forged into a polemic implement which transforms the
academic controversy under debate into a metaphoric struggle
between truth and falsehood. By translating abstract, academic
issues into matters which are personal and felt, Milton makes
them immediate and perceptible to a wide audience. Unlearned
though he may be, the Christian reader can surely understand
that a hierarchy of values has emerged from the interaction of
Scripture and tradition. The wisdom of Scripture is diametrically

opposed to the error of tradition, and neither scholar nor layman can resolve the antithesis. Scripture must remain the final source of truth for Christians. Looking beyond the context of debate for a moment, it is evident that *Prelatical Episcopacy*, like Milton's orations and the *History of Britain*, reduces the issues under discussion to their spiritual essence through the medium of imaginative rhetorical appeals. Theoretically, of course, his appeals ought to prompt the spirits of Anglican scholars and common readers alike, for he has rendered a sectarian theological controversy universally significant. Yet, while decorum demanded that Milton meet his Anglican opponents on their own scholarly grounds, his zeal for Reformation likely led him to believe that the rationalistic methodologies which the Anglicans worked to perfection — methodologies which did not allow for the conviction of the heart — would, ironically, conceal the inner meaning of Christianity from them.

III

The rhetorical circumstances which occasioned *Tetrachordon* resemble to a great extent those which prompted *Prelatical Episcopacy*. *Tetrachordon* is an expansion of the Scriptural commentary Milton offered in the *Doctrine and Discipline of Divorce*, as the preface makes clear: *Doctrine and Discipline*, "as pleas'd some to think, who were thought judicious, had of reason in it to a sufficiencie; what they requir'd, was that the Scriptures there alleg'd, might be discuss'd more fully. To their desires, thus much furder hath been labour'd in the Scriptures. Another sort also who wanted more autorities, and citations, have not been here unthought of" (II, 582). In *Tetrachordon* Milton turns the disputative style to minute Scriptural exegesis. Arnold Williams describes Milton's exegetical method as follows: "Just like scores of commentators, Milton takes up a passage of Scripture, divides it into phrases, sometimes subdivides the phrase into words, and discusses each detail fully. Milton follows the less formal methods of commentary. He uses linguistic analysis and comparison of texts only in a few places. He does not follow the literal exposition of the text by questions, disputations, or problems in the scholastic manner; nor does he add homiletic material by way of moral or allegorical interpretations" (II, 572). Precise textual division, linguistic explication of passages to establish literal and metaphoric meanings, and comparison of Scriptural texts are all assimilated into the disputative mode of *Tetrachordon*. The distinctive structure, dualistic argument, and rhetorical movement of the tract suggest that Milton's exegetical practices are his own, not merely borrowed from one of the numerous commentators he cites. In particular, the centrality of Aristotelian logic and metaphysics in *Tetrachordon* finds a precedent in the *Prolusions* rather than in the scholarly documents Milton is known to have consulted.[99]

Tetrachordon's intention is twofold. Milton is primarily concerned with "the foure chief places in Scripture, which treat of Mariage, or nullities in Mariage": Gen. 1: 27 and 2: 18; Deut. 24: 1-2; Matt. 5: 31-32 and 19: 3-4; and 1 Corin. 7: 10-11. He examines each "place" to verify the thesis that Scripture permits divorce for reasons other than adultery. Like *Prelatical Episcopacy*, *Tetrachordon* is a dialectical disputation, an exploration of the consequences of Milton's position and that of his antagonists, who call for a "literall" reading of Scripture on the divorce question. While the argument of *Prelatical Episcopacy* was essentially a rebuttal, that of *Tetrachordon* is largely affirmative. The brief but lethal refutation passages of the tract are directed at the "common expositors" whom Milton had denounced in the *Doctrine and Discipline*. Milton announces his polemic objective early: "And how injurious herein they are, if not to themselves, yet to their neighbours, and not to them only, but to the all-wise and bounteous grace offer'd us in our redemption, will orderly appear" (II, 587). As it did in *Prelatical Episcopacy*, polemic will translate Milton's scholarly dialectic into universally intelligible terms.

Milton's analysis of Genesis constitutes a sort of preface from which emerges a comprehensive definition of marriage operative throughout the tract. The three remaining sections of *Tetrachordon* are structured in the manner of the *Prolusions*: establishment of the full meaning of the Scriptural text; statement of the problem to be disputed; opinions contrary to Milton's own; arguments in support of his thesis; and answers to the contrary opinions. The interacting modes of proof in Milton's discussion of Genesis resemble those of *Prelatical Episcopacy*:

> It might be doubted why [Genesis] saith, *In the Image of God created he him,* not them, as well as *male and female them;* especially since that Image might be common to them both, but *male and female* could not, however the Jewes fable, and please themselvs with the accidentall concurrence of *Plato's* wit, as if man at first had bin created *Hermaphrodite*: but then it must have bin male and female

created he him. So had the Image of God bin equally common to them both, it had no doubt bin said, In the image of God created he them. But *St. Paul* ends the controversie by explaining that the woman is not primarily and immediatly the image of God, but in reference to the man. *The head of the woman, saith he, I Cor. 11. is the man: he the image and glory of God, she the glory of the man.* (II, 589)

The dialectical process is here brought to bear on a difficult point of Scripture. Milton posits a hypothetical interpretation of the line, and then, using the argument from probability, logically rejects that hypothesis. The specific Scriptural authority of St. Paul resolves the matter, providing Milton with artificial proof of the male-female marital hierarchy.

The explanation of Genesis concludes with a conceptualization of the entire question of marriage in relation to the Aristotelian doctrine of the four causes: "First therfore the material cause of matrimony is man and woman; the Author and efficient, God and their consent, the internal *Form* and the soul of this relation, is conjugal love arising from a mutual fitnes to the final causes of wedlock, help and society in Religious, Civil and Domestic conversation, which includes as an inferior end the fulfilling of natural desire, and specifical increase; these are the final causes both moving the *efficient*, and perfeting the *form*" (II, 608). Having articulated the "problem" in a scholarly manner, Milton reviews "contrary opinions" and evaluates them according to the criteria of the four causes. Logic moves him to repudiate Paraeus' concept of marriage as incoherent and deficient: "*Paraeus* on *Gen.* defines Mariage to be *an indissoluble conjunction of one man and one woman to an individual and intimat conversation, and mutual benevolence* . . . . . . [but] his definition places the ends of Mariage in one order [the spiritual], and esteems them in another [the physical]" (II, 609). The primary flaw in this and other explanations, Milton charges, is that they construct, in direct contradiction to Scripture and reason, a false hierarchy of values in which the spiritual element of marriage is subordinated to the physical.

Consequently, Milton advances his own definition of marriage and defends it in relation to the four causes: "*Mariage is a divine institution joyning man and woman in a love fitly dispos'd to the helps and comforts of domestic life. A divine institution*" (II, 612). An antidote to those of the common expositors, this approach is comprehensive and logical, allowing for the identification of the

proper end of marriage; his definition "contains the prime efficient cause of Mariage . . . . . . Now though efficient causes are not
requisite in a definition, yet divine institution hath such influence
upon the *Form*, and is so a conserving cause of it, that without it
the *Form* is not sufficient to distinguish matrimony from other
conjunctions of male and female, which are not to be counted
mariage" (II, 612). In the idea of consent Milton locates the essence of marriage: "That consent I mean which is a love fitly
dispos'd to mutual help and comfort of life; this is that happy
Form of mariage naturally arising from the very heart of divine
institution in the Text, in all the former definitions either ob-
scurely, and under mistak'n terms exprest, or not at all" (II, 613).

After establishing a sophisticated, academic context of debate
with his scholastic explication of Genesis, Milton proceeds in each
subsequent section of the tract to assimilate the remaining Scriptural texts on marriage into his thesis. His dialectical method
embraces, first, the working out of the consequences of that thesis,
and then a rebuttal of the opponents' positions. As it was in
Prelatical Episcopacy, the argumentative direction of *Tetrachordon* is from logic to evocation. Scholarly rebuttal gives way to
the rhetoric of vehemence as Milton launches an attack on the
common expositors whose doctrines are antithetical to his own.
Since the movement from affirmation through refutation to polemic[100] is virtually identical in the Deuteronomy, Matthew, and
I Corinthians sections of *Tetrachordon*, I have selected Milton's
analysis of Deut. 24: 1-2 for intensive consideration.

His affirmation complete, Milton demolishes the contentions of
the expositors with a logical dialectic reminiscent in its complexity
of the Fourth and Fifth *Prolusions*. Often he brings intricate
syllogisms against them, as in the following case where he denies
that the Scriptural law of marriage sanctions spiritual bondage:

> Fifthly, The Law is to tender the liberty and human dignity
> of them that live under the Law, whether it bee the mans
> right above the woman, or the womans just appeal against
> wrong, and servitude. But the duties of mariage contain in
> them a duty of benevolence, which to doe by compulsion
> against the Soul, where ther can bee neither peace, nor joy,
> nor love, but an enthrallment to one who either cannot, or
> will not bee mutual in the godliest and civilest ends of that
> society, is the ignoblest, and the lowest slavery that a hu-
> man shape can bee put to. This Law therfore justly and
> piously provides against such an unmanly task of bondage
> as this. (II, 625-26)

A corollary of Milton's definition of marriage, the syllogism is, at
the same time, a validation of the definition's internal consistency
and an indictment of the expositors' distortion of Scripture. Milton occasionally concedes points to his opponents but qualifies
the conclusions they have drawn:

> Equity is understood in every Covnant, eevn between en-
> emies, though the terms bee not exprest. If equity therfore
> made it, extremity may dissolv it. But Mariage, they use
> to say, is the Covnant of God. Undoubted: and so is any
> covnant frequently call'd in Scripture, wherin God is call'd
> to witnes: the covnant of freindship between *David* and
> *Jonathan,* is call'd the *Covnant of the Lord,* I Sam. 20 . . .
> . . . . So that this denomination [calling marriage the
> "Covnant of God"] adds nothing to the Covnant of Mariage,
> above any other civil and solemn contract. (II, 624)

Qualification in this instance is supported by specific Scriptural
citation. Milton also denies major premises of the expositors',
countering such premises with a barrage of detailed objections
(e.g., II, 623-25).

Images in *Tetrachordon,* their affective overtones deliberately
subdued, function as examples had functioned in *Prelatical Episcopacy.* Images usually act as non-literal supporting evidence for
theses or as analogues to specific arguments. The following image
buttresses Milton's claim that the style of a Scriptural passage
figures importantly in its meaning: God "would have said, I hate
putting away, saith the Lord; and not sent word by *Malachi* in
a sudden faln stile, *The Lord God saith that hee hateth putting
away*: that were a phrase to shrink the glorious omnipresence of
God . . . . And were as if a Herald in the *Atcheivment* of a King,
should commit the *indecorum* to set his helmet sidewaies and
close, not full fac't and open in the posture of direction and command" (II, 616). Breach of decorum supports the charge that
the expositors amplify the significance of a passage lacking the
distinctive character of divine command.

In order to compel rational assent to his careful re-definition of
marital values, Milton's scholarly rebuttal demands a plain, literal
style. The plain style also assists Milton in establishing the literal meaning of a relevant Scriptural text such as the following:
"[*Because he hath found som uncleannes in her.*] That wee may
not esteem this law to bee a meer authorizing of licence, as the
Pharises took it, *Moses* adds the reason, for *som uncleannes found.*
Som heertofore have bin so ignorant, as to have thought, that this

uncleannes means **adultery**" (II, 620). Imagery or highly affective
diction in the passage might well have created problems of interpretation damaging to his subsequent explication. In the argument from Deuteronomy Milton's style remains, for the most part,
one of academic debate, whose character is established by references to logic, metaphysics, and exegetical commentaries rather
than by vivid imagery.

Yet, as the refutation evolves, Milton's discourse grows evocative. Throughout *Tetrachordon* he had insisted, in opposition to
the expositors who read Deuteronomy's directions literally, that
the "uncleannes" which Scripture recognized as grounds for divorce
might be interpreted as spiritual unfitness or antipathy as well as
adultery. Now, the evocative argument from Deuteronomy reiterates the implications of the expositors' position in universal terms,
demonstrating that the consequences of a literal application of
Deuteronomy's sanctions are spiritual death. The intricate dialectic of *Tetrachordon* is gradually transformed into a satiric weapon
against the expositors. Milton's polemical thrusts correspond to
Wilson's description of the non-logical mode of debate; a sophisticated form of mockery, subsumed under the tropes *Apodioxis* and
Antirrhesis, underlies his attack on the expositors. Milton's ex-
asperated questioning of their dogged adherence to the letter of
the law is, implicitly, an *ad hominem* attack designed to discredit
them: "If mariage may bee dissolv'd by so many exterior powers,
not superior, as wee think, why may not the power of mariage
it self for its own peace and honour dissolv it self, where the persons wedded be free persons, why may not a greater and more
natural power complaining dissolv mariage? for the ends why
matrimony was ordain'd, are certainly and by all Logic above the
Ordinance it self, why may not that dissolv mariage without which
that institution hath no force at all?" (II, 628). The evocative
tempo increases as Milton indicts the corrosive folly of the expositors simply by carrying one of their arguments to its logical conclusion: the husband "might have lookt better before to her
breeding under religious Parents," they charge; "every glaunce of
her eye, every step of her gate would have propheci'd adultery,
if the quick sent of these discerners had bin took along," Milton
answers (II, 629). His *reductio ad absurdum* brands the expositors' position as unrealistic, unable to accommodate human error.
Analogical rebuttal isolates another unfortunate consequence of
their argument: "Let the buyer beware, saith the old Law-beaten
termer. Belike then ther is no more honesty, nor ingenuity in the
bargain of a wedloc, then in the buying of a colt" (II, 630). If

the expositors have their way, the essence of matrimony will inevitably be commercialized.

Clearly, the dignified, scholarly tone of *Tetrachordon* has been displaced by sarcasm and satiric insinuation. Moreover, Milton often sees fit to denounce overtly the evil of his opponents: "But God more mild and good to man, then man to his brother, in all this liberty givn to divorcement, mentions not a word of our past errors and mistakes, if any were, which these men objecting from their own inventions prosecute with all violence and iniquity" (II, 630). This scornful dismissal, reflective of Milton's indignation at the cruelty of the expositors' verdict, demonstrates as well the changed function of ethical proof in the evocative argument. At the outset of his analysis of Deuteronomy, Milton had been concerned with the objective truth or falsehood of the expositors' case, and content simply to identify their positions as correct or incorrect. Now his evaluation grows subjective, personal (aimed at the expositors themselves rather than their position), and explicitly moral. Milton is impelled to brand his antagonists as evil and corrupt, while simultaneously venting his own righteous anger at their perversion of Scripture. Imagery, which had earlier illustrated logical arguments, now becomes primarily an evocative device. Milton's description of the ill-fortuned marriage which "burst like a rott'n thread" is a specimen of pathetic proof, rich in affective, emotional connotations.

The rising tempo of the evocative argument climaxes in a metaphoric exposé of the ignominious spiritual death attendant upon a mistaken reading of Scripture. Milton lists some of the consequences of a false marriage: "dissimulation, suspicion . . . and wors then these, disturbance, annoyance, vexation, sorrow . . . then comes disorder, neglect, hatred, and perpetual strife, all these the enemies of holines and christianity" (II, 631). Afflictions of this sort cannot fail to deaden the spirit of even the strongest Christian; and the malady of false marriage is contagious, contaminating all it touches, whether in the inner circle of the family:

> And wher the houshold stands in this plight, what love can ther bee to the unfortunat issue, what care of thir breeding, which is of main conducement to thir beeing holy (II, 631),

or in the wider sphere of society:

> It degenerates and disorders the best spirits, leavs them . . . unactive to all public service, dead to the Common-wealth. (II, 632)

An intensely personal appeal which draws its strength from the individual Christian's consternation, the metaphoric indictment demands that each reader evaluate the relationship between forced continuance in marriage and the spiritual fabric of the marriage partners.

Unlike the imagistic evocative style of *Prelatical Episcopacy*, *Tetrachordon*'s is rhetorically plain yet impassioned in tone and profoundly suggestive, as in Milton's contrast of his position to that of the expositors: "Therfore God who hates all faining and formality, wher there should bee all faith and sincerenes, and abhorrs to see inevitable discord, wher there should be greatest concord, when through anothers default, faith and concord cannot bee, counts it neither just to punish the innocent with the transgressor, nor holy . . . for the sanctity of mariage . . . to be made the . . . close fight of enmity and hate" (II, 631). Antithetical clauses juxtapose the wisdom of Milton's plea and the vigor of his conviction to the folly of the expositors, while the evocative force of the passage stems from the implicit association of the persona with Scriptural truth.

Thus, the argument from Deuteronomy, which commenced with an erudite, sophisticated textual analysis, ends by revealing the consequences to the individual Christian of a false reading of Scripture. The evocative phase of Milton's discussion resolves the complex issue of divorce into a fundamental opposition between charity and literalism, the spirit of the gospel and the perversion of that spirit, harmony and chaos, happiness and misery. An abstraction, false marriage, is transformed into a deeply personal experience which is apprehensible primarily through the imagination and the emotions, not through logic. That experience is profoundly significant for the layman, and, if he can resist making reason alone responsible for truth, for the scholar as well.

In short, the rhetoric of *Prelatical Episcopacy* and *Tetrachordon* may be explained in relation to the Renaissance tradition of disputation. Both pamphlets are suitable for a learned audience, providing a wealth of technical information for those prepared by training and temperament to assimilate it. Yet the curve of Milton's dialectic is from logic to evocation, from a learned perspective to a popular one. The rhetorical dualism of each tract is surely a tribute to Milton's skill as a polemicist who recognized that dispute would prove fruitless unless the issues he disputed transcended the narrow academic context. More important still, his twofold appeal dramatizes once again a conviction that discourse is most persuasive, most universal, not when it confines itself to the analysis and categorization of speculative reasoning, but when it prompts in the inner man a re-affirmation of basic Christian beliefs.

Sermons in the Plain Style

No phrase is more appropriate than Milton's own, "plane and easie," to describe the style of his pamphlets, *A Treatise of Civil Power in Ecclesiastical Causes* (1659), *Considerations Touching the Likeliest Means to Remove Hirelings out of the Church* (1659), and *The Readie and Easie Way to Establish a Free Commonwealth* (1660).[101] Stylistic movements which engendered the plain prose of Dryden and his contemporaries affected Milton as well. I shall discuss in this chapter the primary characteristics of the aesthetic of plainness so evident in his final major arguments for Christian liberty. I shall also demonstrate how Milton's concern for clarity of discourse includes the dialectic, the structure, and the style of each treatise. What distinguishes the pamphlets of 1659-1660 is surely their plainness, yet *Hirelings* and *The Readie Way* are not uniformly plain. As it did in the other genres we have studied, Milton's rhetoric evolves gradually into polemic, reaching a crescendo in *The Readie Way* when he contemplates the prospect of a restored monarchy. In 1659-1660 Milton thought of his polemic as an expression of Christian freedom which was justified whether it persuaded or not.

Calls for "plane and easie" prose had been sounded from many quarters during the seventeenth century and earlier. The basic explanations for the aesthetic of plainness predominant in the Restoration are familiar. In opposition to Morris Croll's insistence that "anti-Ciceronianism" was the foremost stylistic influence in the seventeenth century, Richard Foster Jones stressed the impact of the new science.[102] Robert Adolph, basically in agreement with Jones, has argued that "Baconian utilitarianism" shaped the Restoration "Prose of Utility."[103] Perry Miller has shown that Ramism contributed to plainness, and Harold Fisch that the Puritans consistently advocated simple prose.[104] J. W. Blench, exploring homiletic literature in greater detail than Fisch did, has discovered plain preaching by both Puritans and Anglicans during the sixteenth century.[105] What is more, the general trend toward simplification and clarification in many areas of life during the first half of the seventeenth century cannot be discounted. To cite but two examples, Sir Edward Coke adapted feudal laws to mercantilist, capitalist society, with much simplifying, while accounts moved from the awkwardness of roman numerals to arabic ones. Evidently, the reasons why plainness eventually triumphed are complex and interrelated: all of the factors cited above, and others, probably contributed to some degree.

Although the origins of "plane and easie" prose remain controversial, there is little doubt that Thomas Sprat voiced the prevailing sentiments of the Restoration when, in 1667, he eulogized the Royal Society's efforts in the matter of style:

> A constant Resolution, to reject all the amplifications, digressions, and swellings of style: to return back to the primitive purity, and shortness, when men deliver'd so many *things*, almost in an equal number of *words*. They have exacted from all their members, a close, naked, natural way of speaking; positive expressions; clear senses; a native easiness: bringing all things as near the Mathematical plainness, as they can: and preferring the language of Artizans, Countrymen, and Merchants, before that, of Wits, or Scholars.[106]

Sprat had announced the normative standard of plainness. Implicit here is the Society's disdain for "specious *Tropes* and *Figures*." According to Sprat and his colleagues, metaphor impeded the primary mission of language, the communication of facts. Involving as it does the creative faculties of the writer, metaphor threatens to distract the reader from factual concerns by stimulating his imagination. The Society's aversion for the non-literal extended to schemes of sound and verbal arrangement, both of which constituted "swellings of style." Alliteration and *chiasmus*, for example, direct attention at the author and away from what he says.

As an alternative to "digressions, and swellings of style," Sprat urged the adoption of the syntactical patterns of modern prose. Cumbersome periodic structures complicated by numerous subordinating conjunctions were to be shunned. Should the writer construct his sentence in the manner of subject-verb-object, he would attain a "native easiness." In order to produce a smooth, linear effect and encourage the reader to examine the nouns in each sentence, individual clauses were to be joined by coordinating conjunctions and by participles such as "having" or "being." Nouns in Restoration prose "stand for fixed, technical concepts, of which everyone has a clear and distinct idea."[107] A typical sentence conforming to Sprat's dictum approximates a series of nouns in juxtaposition, maintained in equilibrium by unemphatic participles. Syntactical units might be likened to a "series of ratios"[108] awaiting addition to achieve complete intelligibility. Finally, Sprat argued that effective expression requires a verbal analogue to the precision of the numerical system, namely brevity.

Sprat's wish that "all things" be brought near the "Mathematical plainness" has equally significant consequences for diction. By eschewing foreign phrases or unusual English words, the writer must purge his diction of the complexity of subjective reaction surrounding it. When one allows the reader to derive as few meanings as possible from any given term, he limits the possibility that an essential idea may be misconstrued. Verbs, in particular, are "chiefly operative, mere markers to indicate distinctions and logical processes to the reader."[109] Forms of "to be," connoting the impersonality of fact, predominate in Restoration writing. Taken collectively, Sprat's sanctions exalt objective description at the expense of personal expression and transform language into a useful medium for the presentation of facts.

The Restoration's liking for clarity encompassed the structure of written discourse as well. John Wilkins' theories about structure in *Ecclesiastes; or a Discourse Concerning the Gift of Preaching as it falls under the rules of Art* (1646) anticipated the thinking of the Restoration. To eradicate the often perplexing multiple fragmentations of the Scriptural text characteristic of Anglican and Puritan sermons alike, Wilkins proposed a tripartite sermon arrangement. Religious writing ought to consist of an explication of the general meaning of the text; a confirmation, or opening out of the single theme which arose from the text by means of "strong Logicall consequences" and testimony "both human and divine"; and an application of the theme to the life of the Christian.[110] The reader's attention was thereby focused on the sustained development of a single idea. Wilkins' concept of structure was widely favored by Restoration divines.[111] Milton, too, came to recognize the advantages of precisely structured discourse.

The concluding paragraph of *Civil Power* summarizes Milton's rhetorical strategy in that tract as well as in *Hirelings* and *The Readie Way*: "in matters of religion he is learnedest who is planest. The brevitie I use . . . will not therfore, I suppose, be thought the less considerable . . . . I rather chose the common rule, not to make much ado where less may serve. Which in controversies and those especially of religion, would make them less tedious, and by consequence read ofter, by many more, and with more benefit" (VI, 41). Milton's ideals resemble closely those arrived at later in Sprat's credo. Milton's profound sensitivity to his intellectual milieu would surely have acquainted him with the evolving aesthetic of plainness. His works of 1659-1660 may, in fact, be viewed as significant contributions to the development of that aesthetic. In the plain style Milton found an effective means of reaching an audience grown increasingly receptive to the clarity and "ease" of what was to become the Restoration idiom.

Of primary concern to Milton in the last tracts are the "matters of religion" to which he referred above. From each pamphlet emerges a distinct aspect of a simplified Christian religion purged of externals through a constant reductive process. Milton isolates thereby the personal, ecclesiastical, and political consequences of the indispensable principle in the Christian dispensation, the freedom of the inner man. Inner freedom is the essence of that liberty which Milton claimed was fundamental to his polemic labors. *Civil Power, Hirelings,* and *The Readie Way* deal, respectively, with the themes of "personal," "ecclesiastical," and "civil" liberty issuing from St. Paul's Epistle to the Corinthians: *"the spiritual man judgeth all things, but he himself is judgd of no man"* (VI, 7-8). The plainness of these pamphlets adumbrates Milton's changed conception of the audience for whom he wrote. The Miltonic vision of universal spiritual concord integral to treatises such as *Areopagitica* has narrowed.[112]

The collapse of the Revolution convinced Milton that Reformation for all the people was unattainable. Milton recognized also that in 1659-1660 he must be practical in order to persuade. Hence he does not argue for national and international Reformation, but only for a political system that would perform what he considered minimal tasks: preserve law and order, keep church and state separate, and allow spiritual integrity to the individual. Clearly, the time for stirring visions of Revolution accomplished had passed. Realizing that he fought a rearguard action, Milton abandoned the complex rhetoric of his earlier works in favor of presenting the plain truth — at a critical time — to a nation grown skeptical and disillusioned after nearly two decades of turmoil. Yet Milton wrote in 1659-1660 for the few as well as for the many. In all three pamphlets he spoke to those whose regenerate sensibility would allow them to grasp the full implications of Christian liberty. His purpose in so doing was to alert the regenerate to the ways in which they could realize the spiritual harmony of the "paradise within."

In *Civil Power* the plain style defines the sacred spiritual identity of the regenerate Christian, and the rational clarity of Milton's argument is implemented by the tract's structural pattern. It is divided into three distinct parts, approximating the explication, confirmation, and application advised by Wilkins. The explication presents the theme of inner liberty together with the Scriptural text which justifies such liberty:

Whence I here mean by conscience or religion, that full perswasion whereby we are assur'd that our beleef and practise, as far as we are able to apprehend and probably make appeer, is according to the will of God and his Holy Spirit within us, which we ought to follow much rather then any law of man, as not only his word every where bids us, but the very dictate of reason tells us. *Act.* 4. 19. *whether it be right in the sight of God, to hearken to you more then to God, judge ye.* (VI, 5)

A confirmation in the form of four distinct arguments follows the explication. Milton maintains that: Scripture, the sole criterion of truth for Protestants, guarantees the sanctity of the individual conscience; although a civil magistrate may be *able* to judge in matters of conscience he has no *right*, for his jurisdiction extends only to civil matters; not only can the civil power do no good in matters of religion, but it does violence to the "new birthright of everie true believer, Christian libertie"; finally, punishing nonbelievers or compelling them in any way affronts God. Each subdivision is an autonomous unit combining both confirmation and refutation, and each is afforded a single lengthy paragraph in the text. Digressions of any sort are absent and the seeming redundancy of argument is in fact a testimony to the meticulous development of the single theme set out in the explication. *Civil Power* concludes with a brief, generalized application which epitomizes the meaning Milton expects to be derived from the confirmation: "As to those magistrates who think it their work to settle religion, and those ministers or others, who so oft call upon them to do so, I trust, that having well considered what hath bin here argu'd, neither they will continue in that intention, nor these in that expectation from them" (VI, 39). To insure the clarity of his presentation, Milton informs the reader of the major structural divisions in the text when they occur, as in the following case: "I have shewn that the civil power hath neither right nor can do right by forcing religious things: I will now shew the wrong it doth" (VI, 28). Within the four main theses of the tract, clarity is achieved through enthymemes which act as a means of recapitulation and transition among the sections of each argument.[113] Constantly Milton reminds the reader of the distinct relationships among all structural units of the treatise. One perceives in *Civil Power* a group of individual parts clearly related instead of a blurred totality.

All non-essentials are stripped away from the Christian religion by the dialectical mode of *Civil Power*. The reductive action applies to Milton's comprehensive definition of religion ("What evangelic religion is, is told in two words, faith and charitie; or beleef and practice"), and to his understanding of principal concepts. Thus he redefines "heresie":

> They [Milton's opponents] should first interpret [to the people], that heresie, by what it signifies in that language [Greek], is no word of evil note; meaning only the choise or following of any opinion good or bad in religion or any other learning. (VI, 11)

By paring down a "Greek apparition" and its confusing associations to "plain" English ones ("any opinion good or bad"), Milton thwarts the efforts of those who resort to verbal ambiguity to mislead the regenerate. Within each argument reductive forces also operate. Again and again, Milton derives the simplest possible meaning from a Scriptural text, as he does below in dealing with the question of civil power: "*Wilt thou then not be affraid of the power? do that which is good and thou shalt have praise of the same.* This shews that religious matters are not here meant; wherin from the power here spoken of they could have no praise" (VI, 15). Lengthy explication might distract the reader from the universal clarity of Scripture. The terminal stage of the reductive process is a form of non-argument. Rather than belaboring the matter of interpretation, Milton frequently does no more than quote a text for the reader's perusal. For Milton, plainness, brevity, and simplicity are equivalent to truth. His reductive dialectic parallels Sprat's linguistic dictum that so many "*things*" be contained in an equal number of "*words*."

Milton's style makes public the Christian truth asserted by his argument. In its fluid directness, the syntax of *Civil Power* differs fundamentally from the knotty Latinate patterns, represented here by *Of Reformation*, of Milton's early works:

> Amidst those deepe and retired thoughts, which with every man Christianly instructed, ought to be most frequent, of *God*, and of his miraculous *ways*, and *works*, amongst men, and of our *Religion* and *Worship*, to be perform'd to him; after the story of our Saviour *Christ*, suffering to the lowest bent of weaknesse, in the *Flesh*, and presently triumphing to the highest pitch of *glory*, in the *Spirit*, which drew up his body also, till we in both be united to him in the Revelation of his Kingdome: I do not know of any thing more worthy to take up the whole passion of pitty, on the one side, and

> joy on the other: then to consider first, the foule and sudden corruption, and then after many a tedious age, the long-deferr'd, but much more wonderfull and happy reformation of the *Church* in these latter dayes. (*CP*, I, 519)

This citation exemplifies the syntactical arrangement of *Civil Power*:

> First it cannot be deni'd, being the main foundation of our protestant religion, that we of these ages, having no other divine rule or autoritie from without us warrantable to one another as a common ground but the holy scripture, and no other within us but the illumination of the Holy Spirit so interpreting that scripture as warrantable only to our selves and to such whose consciences we can so perswade, can have no other ground in matters of religion but only from the scriptures. (VI, 6)

Smoothness and linearity stand out in the syntax of the second passage. Its members are joined by detachable participles which enclose a simple declarative sentence ("it cannot be denied . . . that we . . . can have") in the manner of subject-verb-object. The Latinate periodicity of the first example circles around the notion of the Resurrection, amplifying the subject matter with schemes of sound and repetition,[114] but the latter proceeds directly to a factual conclusion. Instead of embellishing the subject, its participial phrases advance supporting evidence for the stated fact. The centrality of "being" and "having," which attest to little more than the fact of existence, further emphasizes the factual character of the second passage. In each phrase, nouns and coordinate conjunctions connecting them arrest the reader's attention. When one assembles the "series of ratios" Milton presents, he arrives at a verification of the Scriptural basis of Protestantism. In opposition to the personal verbal assertion in *Of Reformation* ("I do not know"), *Civil Power* displays an impersonal, dogmatic one ("it cannot be deni'd"). The syntactical features of *Civil Power* place the reader in close contact with significant facts, not personal reactions.

In the interests of "brevitie," moreover, Milton has recourse to an unprecedented number of concise, summarily direct sentences such as this: "What I argue, shall be drawn from the scripture only; and therin from true fundamental principles of the gospel; to all knowing Christians undeniable" (VI, 4). He permits no more "*words*" than necessary to convey the "*things*" of his argument. Not only are "digressions" and "swellings" of any sort which would lengthen the sentence absent, but the adjectives "true" and "fundamental" are agents of logical distinction rather than rhetorical amplification.[115]

A most effective way of clarifying the truth of Christian liberty is the banishment of what Sprat termed "specious *Tropes and Figures.*" In the Milton canon *Civil Power* stands alone for its paucity of simile and metaphor. The metaphoric ingenuity of the following selection from *Of Prelatical Episcopacy* is alien to the treatise:

> Whatsoever time, or the heedlesse hand of blind chance, hath drawne down from of old to this present, in her huge drag-net, whether Fish, or Sea-weed, Shells, or Shrubbs, unpickt, unchosen, those are the Fathers. (*CP*, I, 626)

In *Civil Power* fact replaces metaphor:

> Two things there be which have bin ever found working much mischief to the church of God, and the advancement of truth; force on the one side restraining, and hire on the other side corrupting the teachers thereof. (VI, 4)

Numerically specific, Milton's objective claim invites not emotive, but rational appraisal. The affective power of metaphor has yielded to the denotive, colorless precision of mathematical predication.

In the diction of *Civil Power* can be found a Miltonic version of the "Mathematical plainness," the "clear senses" representative of semantic certainty for Sprat. The austerity of *Civil Power* departs radically from the graphic vitality of a tract such as the *Animadversions upon the Remonstrants Defence against Smectymnuus* (1641):

> After all [the prelates'] Monkish prohibitions, and *expurgatorious* indexes, your *gags* and *snaffles* . . . not to be obtain'd without the shallow surview, but not shallow hand of some mercenary, narrow Soul'd, and illitterate Chaplain; when liberty of speaking . . . was girded, and straight lac't almost to a broken-winded *tizzick*. (*CP*, I, 669; my italics)

The *Animadversions* demonstrates how an energetic polemic vocabulary generates diverse emotional reactions. Polemic imagination dictates Milton's choice of a Latinate word ("expurgatorious") and the obsolete form of an Anglo-Saxon word ("tizzick"). Diction of this kind blazons forth the creative temperament of the author and, while communicating the universal sentiments of anger and disgust, remains highly personal. In contrast, *Civil Power* is "plane and easie": "That Christ is the only lawgiver of his church and that it is here meant in religious matters, no well grounded Christian will deny" (VI, 8). Milton's diction has now become common, primarily Anglo-Saxon, largely devoid of suggestive force, and hence fully intelligible. It shields the author behind a barrier of linguistic anonymity. As he does consistently throughout the tract, Milton again forsakes the wide-ranging allusiveness of his early prose; the "words" of Scripture are sufficient. Milton's simplification of his own diction justifies his condemnation of those who rely upon sophisticated "Greek" terms to mislead the reader.

To speed the dialectical flow of the pamphlet, Milton reduces to insignificance the role of authorial persona. In tracts as rhetorically intricate as *Areopagitica*, an authorial persona carefully controls reader reaction, while in *Civil Power* the persona is diminutive. Above all, he seeks to offer the reader factual truth and to allow him full judgment on those facts. Frequently Milton distances himself not only from the act of judgment, but from the very texts which comprise his argument, insisting at one point that "my inference is, or rather not mine but our Saviours own," that in matters of civil power in religion, civil magistrates "neither can command nor use constraint" (VI, 9). As a result of authorial non-involvement, the reader confronts the truth of Scripture directly.[116]

The style of *Civil Power* makes "plane" the sacred identity of the regenerate Christian, the consequence of "the spirit of God itself within us." Clearly, Scripture forbids the civil magistrate to trespass upon the domain of the conscience. Milton's arguments provide, therefore, a rationale for Parliament, the audience to whom *Civil Power* is ostensibly addressed, to preserve the inner liberty charted in the tract. But the meaning of *Civil Power* for the individual regenerate reader is at least as important as its meaning for the legislature. Whether or not Parliament follows Milton's advice, he has appealed forcefully to the spiritual awareness of each regenerate Christian. Despite its plainness and brevity, *Civil Power* abounds in implications realizable within the individual conscience alone. After the reader has contemplated the truth of Christian liberty, he must apply it as completely as his own state of regeneracy allows. Awareness of one's sacred identity permits him to recognize his spiritual enemies, no matter how subtle their disguises, and renders unnecessary ponderous tomes on the dangers to the Christian religion.

Milton explores in *Civil Power* themes largely public and utilitarian in nature, but not completely so. In the opening pages of his discussion he mentions truth of another kind: "however to the truth [*Civil Power*] will be at all times no unneedfull testimonie; at least some discharge of that general dutie which no Christian but according to what he hath receivd, knows is requir'd of him" (VI, 5). In effect, Milton attaches personal significance to the Christian duty of bearing witness. Public and personal truth are united in *Civil Power* by the mechanics of self-definition. In the process of vindicating the sacred identity of all regenerate Christians, Milton simultaneously affirms his own. Writing is transformed into a symbolic act of self-assertion whereby Milton testifies to the existence of his inner freedom. If Milton expounded the truth of Christian liberty in *Civil Power,* his regenerate self will testify in *Hirelings* and *The Readie Way* to truths often bitter.

II

The thesis of *Hirelings* derives from the premise of liberty postulated in *Civil Power*: ministers are to be valued only insofar as they are responsive to the needs of the inner man. Christ and the Apostles are reliable models of the minister's basic rights and obligations. After the fashion of St. Paul, the Christian divine must earn his own livelihood. Insistence upon tithes and compulsory maintenance is the act of a hireling who worships externals — money and comfort — in place of God.

The structure of Milton's argument is again tripartite. The explication defines the problem of hire:

> That which makes [hire] so dangerous in the church, and properly makes the *hireling*, a word always of evil signification, is either the excess thereof, or the undue manner of giving and taking it (VI, 48),

citing the appropriate Scriptural texts as evidence:

> *Acts* 20. 29. *For, I know this, that after my departing shall greevous wolves enter in among you, not sparing the flock.* Tit. 1. 11. *Teaching things which they ought not, for filthy lucres sake.* 2 Pet. 2. 3. *And through covetousnes shall they with feigned words make merchandise of you.* (VI, 49)

The confirmation of the tract then explains how hirelings ought to be dealt with, its argument falling into three clearly differentiated phases, each of which, in a separate paragraph in the text, includes both affirmation and rebuttal. The brief application re-directs the reader to the tract's major premise: "Of which hireling crew together with all the mischiefs, dissentions, troubles . . . Christendom might soone rid herself and be happie, if Christians would but know thir own dignitie, thir libertie, thir adoption . . . thir spiritual priesthood, whereby they have all equally access to any ministerial function whenever calld by thir own abilities and the church" (VI, 99).

Through devices similar to those of *Civil Power*, chiefly the explicit declaration of substantive changes in the movement of the thesis, and the use of enthymemes as vehicles of résumé and transition, Milton attains structural clarity in *Hirelings*. Each of the discrete, self-contained units of argument in the confirmation reaches its particular conclusion before the pivotal contention of the tract (that hirelings ought to be removed) proceeds.[117] This dialectical method diverges from that of an oration such as *Areopagitica* which, because it diffuses its arguments over one extensive confirmation and brief, intermittent refutations, must link the arguments rhetorically to aid the reader's memory. In *Areopagitica* an elaborate aggregate of dialectic, often interrupted by digressions, looms before the reader, whereas in *Hirelings* several distinct divisions are presented to him.

Direct statement of Scripture connotes plainness in *Hirelings* as it did in *Civil Power*. Whenever possible Milton merely quotes pertinent texts, for instance, those treating the maintenance of ministers.[118] On occasion he intervenes between reader and Scripture, but only to simplify a possibly ambiguous passage. Authorial function is confined to illustrating the clarity and consistency of Scripture on the question of the ministry. Milton refrains from exegetical maneuvering, for his ends are better served by reiterating in as many dialectical contexts as possible the New Testament passages relevant to the Christian priesthood (especially Acts and I Corinthians), in the hope that the reader will resolve the issue for himself.

Finally, as he does here, Milton sets forth in the plain style Scripture's verdict on the ministerial debate: "Next, it is as cleer in the same chapter, that the priests and Levites had not tithes for their labor only in the tabernacle, but in regard they were to have no other part nor inheritance in the land, *Vers.* 20, 24. and by that means for a tenth lost a twelfth" (VI, 52). Presented impersonally and with affirmative sureness, Milton's factual assertion may be verified by consulting the verse of Scripture cited. The linear syntax of *Civil Power*, with its subject-verb-object progression, noun-centered ratios, and verbal neutrality, reappears in *Hirelings*. Evident too is the "Mathematical plainness" of Milton's diction, his avoidance of tropes and schemes. Confident that Scripture is "clear," Milton chooses to be unobtrusive. His purpose of speaking freely in a public debate to inspire laws most advantageous for Christian liberty is fulfilled by the plain style. Surely that style would appeal to the regenerate reason of some parliamentarians who might wish to implement his proposals. More importantly, Milton admonishes the reader to heed Christ's call for the priesthood of all believers. To abolish the sway of hirelings over them, men need only accept the responsibilities of their Christian priesthood.

Even though *Hirelings* approaches *Civil Power* in its clear manifestation of public truth, the regenerate self finds a new direction in the later pamphlet. Milton again emphasizes the gravity of bearing personal witness: "And if there be among them [hirelings] who hold it thir duty to speak impartial truth . . . let them not envie others who think the same no less their duty by the general office of Christianity" (VI, 48). In *Hirelings* the regenerate self testifies to the dichotomy between Scriptural mandates on the ideals of the ministry and the corrupt practices of hirelings. Milton cries out against the evil of the rapacious "wolves" alluded to in Scripture.

As each major argument closes, the voice of regeneracy reaches a crescendo. Having disclosed the need for a priesthood concerned with the inner man, Milton is moved to lament the failure of human response. Often his testimony exposes the twisted logic of hirelings: "For to what purpose do they bring these trivial testimonies, by which they might as well prove altars, candles at noone, and the greatest part of those superstitions . . . which the Papist . . . retains to this day?" (VI, 65). Scornful dismissal of hirelings' claims is another means of branding such claims as perverse: "The last and lowest sort of thir arguments, that men purchas'd not thir tithe with thir land and such like pettifoggerie, I omitt; as refuted sufficiently by others" (VI, 67). Milton's most compelling attacks are his frequent, ominous predictions of the punishment God will mete out to hirelings:

> But what can be planer Simonie, then thus to be at charges beforehand to no other end then to make thir ministry doubly or trebly beneficial? to whom it might be said as justly as to that *Simon, thy monie perish with thee, because thou hast thought that the gift of God may be purchas'd with monie: thou hast neither part nor lot in this matter.* (VI, 93)

In the argumentative contexts which support them, Milton's polemical thrusts combine with his positive assertions to illuminate a larger truth of which human evil must necessarily be a part. As the following citation shows, affective, emphatic syntax and a strident tone characterize the style of witness:

> I omitt also [hirelings'] violent and irreligious exactions . . . thir seising of pots and pans from the poor . . . from som, the very beds; thir sueing and imprisoning; worse then when those wicked sons of *Eli* were priests, whose manner was thus to seise thir pretended priestly due by force. (VI, 67-68)

Harsh participles and verbs ("seise," "sueing," "imprisoning") offer a striking contrast to the "being" and "having" of the public style. Milton deliberately selects a biblical allusion for its evocative power, and his irate tone is far removed from bland factuality. Analogues to the style of witness occur in the slashing invective of earlier pamphlets we have examined. It is essential to recognize, however, that the polemic of *Hirelings* is neither a rhetorical ploy nor a means of winning assent to Milton's position, but rather the "dutie of a Christian to offer what his conscience perswades him." Irrespective of the persuasive force of one's rhetoric, this duty must be undertaken.

In accordance with Milton's exercise of his prerogative of testifying, a personal element informs the style of witness. Yet the regenerate persona is couched in generalities at the outset of *Hirelings* (he is one of "others" who seek to speak the truth), and in prophetic language at the end: "If I be not heard nor beleevd, the event will bear me witnes to have spoken truth" (VI, 100). Milton's personal identity is subsumed, in the first instance, to that of a typological response to evil, the response of all regenerate men. In the second, the persona's apocalyptic exclamations associate him with a prophet, the result being that the reader's attention focuses not upon the prophet but upon his prophecy. When Milton speaks, he gives evidence of the Holy Spirit within him; his testament is both personal and emblematic. The voice of witness proclaims profound moral truths to the regenerate reader.

III

Milton concerns himself in *The Readie Way* with the effect of civil liberty upon Christian freedom. Just as the companion tracts had outlined the hazards of oppressive external forces to the inner

man, *The Readie Way* outlines the dangers to Christian liberty
from gentilism. For the Christian, excessive contact with the
"gentiles" who inhabit the outer kingdom beyond the spiritual
boundaries of Christianity might cause retrogression into gentilish
unregeneracy.[119] In the England of 1660, Milton contends, the
legions of gentilism are poised to usurp the liberty of the saints
and inaugurate a reign of spiritual slavery. Encompassing the civil
tyranny Milton had argued against in *Civil Power* and the ecclesiastical tyranny he had decried in *Hirelings*, the tyranny of gentilish kingship will be universal. Milton names his audience in
The Readie Way as "those who yield not," those who yearn for
freedom and abhor the gentilish practice of kingship. To this regenerate minority he will reveal the way of salvation.

For the most part, however, Milton must bear witness to a
chaotic prospect: the imminent Restoration of a Stuart. In the
second edition of *The Readie Way*, which may be divided into
three parts, as were the earlier tracts, the regenerate self emerges
as the dominant voice.[120] Milton censures in the first section the
vices of kingship, pleads in the second for the free commonwealth,
and forecasts in the third the evil about to engulf England. Each
partition reflects a different Miltonic reaction to the unfolding plot
of history.[121]

In the opening third of *The Readie Way* the regenerate self is
caught up in the chaos it details as Milton narrates England's
heroic break with monarchy and its present desire to embrace
slavery:

> And the dangers on either side [earnest parliamentarians]
> thus waighd: from the treatie, short fruits of long labours
> and seaven years warr; securitie for twenty years . . . then
> put to shift again with our vanquishd maister. His justice
> his honour, his conscience declar'd quite contrarie to ours;
> which would have furnishd him with many such evasions, as
> in a book entitl'd *an inquisition for blood*, soon after were
> not conceald: bishops not totally remov'd, but left as it
> were in ambush, a reserve, with ordination in thir sole powr;
> thir lands alreadie sold, not to be alienated, but rented, and
> the sale of them call'd *sacrilege* . . . accessories punishd; the
> chief author, above pardon, though after utmost resistance,
> vanquish'd; not to give, but to receive laws; yet besought,
> treated with, and to be thankd for his gratious concessions,
> to be honourd, worshipd, glorifi'd. (VI, 115)

An allusion to the Treaty of Newport, which the King and Parliament tried to negotiate in 1647-1648, begins the intricate passage.[122] The King's treacherous "evasions" betokened peril, and the historical patterns of thirteen years ago, Milton intimates, parallel those of today. Lurching forward on a succession of present participles, the disordered syntax fuses time and events, creating the impression that England is about to encounter disaster, as it did a decade earlier. All is reduced, by the purposeful confusion of times and places, to the common denominator of chaos, until Milton's final words ("to be honourd, worshipd, glorifi'd") seem to foretell an impending reality. His witness has become symbolic. Paralyzed by the sheer immensity and momentum of happenings heralding the approach of apocalypse, the regenerate self is bewildered. Its utterances are fragmentary, elliptical, at times half-completed thoughts, a testament to the irrational commotion swirling about it.

The voice of witness rages in vain, throughout the second partition of the treatise, at the maelstrom it had depicted before. Rancor and outrage vent themselves in scathing denunciation:

> Can the folly be paralleld, to adore and be the slaves of a single person for doing that which it is ten thousand to one whether he can or will do, and we without him might do more easily, more effectually, more laudably our selves? . . . Is it such an unspeakable joy to serve, such felicitie to wear a yoke? to clink our shackles, lockt on by pretended law of subjection more intolerable and hopeless to be ever shaken off, then those which are knockt on by illegal injurie and violence. (VI, 136)

At the same time that images of slavery fill the passage, the involuted syntax signifies the "folly" and turmoil Milton anticipates. His disgust is evident, but the dominant tone is one of amazement. National eagerness for the certain tyranny of a Stuart confounds the regenerate self. On other occasions, Milton lashes out bitterly at those he considers responsible for bringing a catastrophe upon the nation:

> Let our zealous backsliders forethink now with themselves, how thir necks yok'd with these tigers of Bacchus . . . inspir'd with nothing holier then the Venereal pox, can draw one way under monarchie to the establishing of church discipline with these new-disgorg'd atheismes: yet shall they not have the honor to yoke with these, but shall be yok'd under them; these shall plow on their backs. (VI, 139)

The "zealous" Presbyterians will be consumed by the gluttonous beasts they have unleashed. Yoking imagery and satiric diction represent the fury of violent, animalistic passions, the triumph of unregeneracy soon to follow.

Milton's most emphatic testimony is located in the last section of *The Readie Way* and summed up in the familiar lines:

> What I have spoken, is the language of that which is not call'd amiss *the good Old Cause*: if it seem strange to any, it will not seem more strange, I hope, then convincing to backsliders. Thus much I should perhaps have said though I were sure I should have spoken only to trees and stones; and had none to cry to, but with the Prophet, *O earth, earth, earth!* to tell the very soil it self, what her perverse inhabitants are deaf to. Nay though what I have spoke, should happ'n . . . to be the last words of our expiring libertie.
> (VI, 148)

Earlier Milton had envisioned chaos as impending; now he treats it as fact. Verbs in the past and future tenses have supplanted present participles, implying that past decisions have set in motion forces which must inevitably culminate in future calamity, forces which present actions are virtually powerless to influence. Hence the tone of the passage is detached and a sense of pure irony pervades it. Milton simply states the disparity between visionary ideal and sordid reality. The despairing finality evinced by Milton's comparison of himself with Jeremiah is epitomized in the final sentence of the tract where he laments the "torrent also of the people" and the "precipice of destruction" over which the "deluge" of their "epidemic madness" threatens to hurl all of England. The images of a rampaging flood connote anarchy already begun. Events of stunning magnitude and swiftness have diminished the voice of the regenerate self to an empty whisper of futility. Intensely personal though it is, Milton's response to apocalypse embodies the paralysis, anger, and weary resignation of all the regenerate toward their common woe.

Disillusionment does not, however, deter Milton from recommending a means to avert pandemonium. Social stability and a provident system of political and moral values would be guaranteed in the commonwealth he advocates. Man's essential freedoms, "liberty of conscience" and "the civil rights and advancements of every person according to his merit," would be protected. When Milton denounced monarchy he did so with a disordered polemical style, but when he tenders his proposal for a republic plainness prevails. In *The Readie Way* the plain style is synonymous with order, rationality, and hierarchy. Brevity and clarity are important elements of persuasion, providing a firm buttress for the plan itself. Here Milton explains why the nation's "Grand or General Councel . . . should be perpetual": "The day of counsel cannot be set as the day of a festival; but must be readie alwaies to prevent or answer all occasions" (VI, 126). Compact and unambiguous, his remark echoes the subject-verb-object paradigm, coordinate linkage, and precise, factual diction of *Civil Power* and *Hirelings*. Milton has pronounced a public truth in language unmistakably clear.

Although the commonwealth holds out a plausible escape from tragedy, there is abundant evidence that Milton doubted its effectiveness on a national scale. He surely knew that the very Parliament upon which he based the perpetual senate would probably favor the Restoration. Even if he did not, the despairing testament of the regenerate self questions the likelihood of a dramatic reversal in popular sentiment. To regenerate Christians, however, the concept of the commonwealth is immeasurably significant. The principles underlying Milton's plan have both a personal and a public application, for guidelines designed to assure political harmony can also assure spiritual harmony. Essential to Milton's government is the exercise of regenerate reason. Just as right reason would encourage the choice of a perpetual Council to preserve political concord, it would encourage concord in the individual soul. Regenerate reason can create a proper hierarchy of moral values as well as political ones. Not only could regenerate reason hasten the establishment of a state secure until the Second Coming, but it could likewise preserve spiritual order until each soul's confrontation with Christ in death. Milton claims that provisions would be made in the republic for spiritual and civil liberty. In the individual soul regeneracy would lead each Christian to comprehend and apply the personal ramifications of Christian liberty by fostering an awareness of his sacred identity. For the regenerate, then, the laws of the free government might be of assistance in ruling the inner kingdom. Even though the Commonwealth of the Saints was soon to be overrun, it was sufficient for Milton in 1660 that its values live on in the spirit of every believer.

As I have demonstrated, Milton's rhetorical objectives in the pamphlets of 1659-1660 were twofold. Attempting to spell out the implications of Christian liberty for the nation and for the regenerate reader, Milton wrote plainly in the prose style and structural format which were to rise to prominence in the Restoration. Although his hopes for Reformation of church and state were diminished in the last tracts, he remained confident that the individual conscience could withstand all external threats to its integrity. But Milton's plea for the realization of Christian freedom did not blind him to the neglect and denial of it. With his voice of witness he cried out against present evils and those certain to afflict England in the future. Because his prophetic witness is an idealized expression of Christian liberty, a voice which refuses to be still when trying circumstances have intimidated others into silence, its impact is regenerative. Yet, while spiritual regeneration undoubtedly concerned Milton in 1659-1660, he likewise responded to the pressing need to profess doctrines beyond the limits of rhetoric, Christian truths which merited speaking whether men heeded them or not.

Harmony and Discord

It has been my principal contention in this study that Milton's major arguments for Christian liberty were presented in several distinct genres of Renaissance prose. The rhetorical conventions of those genres are evident in the tracts I have examined. Equally evident is the fact that Milton understood the conventions well enough to modify them, when necessary, in order to state the case for liberty more effectively. The apocalyptic high style of *Areopagitica* and the disputative mode of *Prelatical Episcopacy* and *Tetrachordon* are two prominent instances of such modification: Milton made the formulae of classical oratory and of Renaissance disputation advance the cause of Reformation. What is more, one can see in Milton's orations and disputations how his academic exercises affected his practices as a polemicist, for both genres are anticipated in the *Prolusions*. Milton utilized his Cambridge training with maximum effectiveness when he entered the political turmoil of the 1640's. In addition, Milton's mastery of all the genres I have analyzed demonstrates his artistry in prose fully as much as his sonnets and epics demonstrate artistry in poetry. During the prose period Milton fulfilled his commitment in *The Reason of Church-Government* (I, 812-23) not merely to imitate literary tradition, but to enrich it in whatever ways his talents dictated.

Secondly, I have shown that, although the process differs somewhat with each genre, Milton's rhetoric inevitably proceeds from public to personal. In successive tracts within a given mode, his method of argument changes from logic to evocation, while detached, factual stances eventually give way to polemic vehemence. Throughout his pamphleteering career Milton remained faithful to the idea that the poet must be a "true poem." And the rhetorician must seek the conviction of the heart, not simply the assent of the intellect. Yet a number of modifications in the public-to-personal paradigm are significant too. Although Milton's polemic is usually imagistic, symbols largely supplant images in *The Tenure* and *Tetrachordon*. Because of Milton's reliance upon the evocative context of Scripture in these two pamphlets, symbols perform the affective functions ordinarily reserved for images. Occasionally, as in the treatises of 1659-1660 and in the *History of Britain*, ironic statements diminish the intensity of Milton's polemic. The rhetori-

cal rationale behind the polemic of 1659-1660 differs considerably
from the rationale of earlier years. Milton's rhetoric of vehemence
finally became a means of bearing witness to truths his countrymen had scorned in their perverse yearnings for slavery. Polemic
could no longer persuade the nation in 1659-1660.

It is likewise apparent that Milton's prose gradually evolved
from ornateness and complexity into austerity and directness. Ornateness occurs in many forms during the 1640's, for example, the
stylistic pageantry of *Areopagitica* and the intricate dialectical interplay of *Prelatical Episcopacy*. By 1649, however, plainness had
become increasingly obvious. The books of the *History* composed
between 1645 and 1649 display a linear, economical style. *The
Tenure* is a symbolical work, but it is less complicated stylistically
than *Areopagitica* was. Simplicity of argument, structure, style,
and persona was Milton's credo in 1659-1660; for aesthetic and
pragmatic reasons he rejected the rhetorical sophistication and
flourish of his earlier works.

Finally, the rhetoric of the prose period provides some insight
into Milton's changing conception of liberty and of those worthy
to possess it. Considerable attention has been paid to the historical
and political factors responsible for constricting Milton's once
expansive vision of Christian liberty.[123] Milton gradually came to
concede that liberty is not in itself a panacea for moral, political,
and ecclesiastical crises, but only a condition necessarily antece-
dent to a solution.[124] To the end, Milton insisted that liberty is
the property of the regenerate, yet his estimate of the number of
the regenerate was far different in 1660 than it was in the anti-
prelatical tracts and in *Areopagitica*. The "fit audience" capable
of perceiving the full implications of *The Readie Way* was small
indeed. Milton's lengthy career in the service of Christian liberty
ended with the sobering realization that the Holy Community
with its transcendent union of individual, church, and state could
not be attained on this earth. Despite that sobering realization,
Milton held on to his belief that liberty as a dynamic interior
condition could lead individuals on to unlimited spiritual growth
and discovery in all times and places. Individuals would, in fact,
strengthen their hold on liberty in direct proportion to the intensity of the trials that beset them on the way to the Heavenly
Jerusalem.

The expansion and ultimate contraction of Milton's vision are
thrown into sharper relief when we compare the rhetorical patterns of the 1640's pamphlets discussed in this study to those of
the 1650's. In the 1640's Milton's stance toward liberty and

Reformation was harmonious, public, and immediate. Nowhere is Milton's optimism more vibrant than in *Areopagitica* where his lengthiest argument is a prophetic, inspiring celebration of England's potential for Reformation, of the eventual founding of the New Jerusalem. The rhetoric of *Areopagitica* intimates the harmony which will prevail when warring "schisms and sects" join forces against the age-old enemies of Reformation. Especially in the peroration, Milton's style symbolically harmonizes past and present, ideal and actual, the Providential design and human reaction to it. The prophet's people are "noble and puissant." Although not so radiant, *The Tenure* is nevertheless hopeful: Milton "was holding fast to that idea of England as a nation of worthies and sages, the humanist New Jerusalem, the godly republic which he had urged upon Parliament in *Areopagitica* in 1644 and which he now expected to be realized under the Commonwealth."[125] Confident of the inherent right of the English people to moral and political freedom, Milton devotes the oration's powerfully evocative peroration to a forward glance at the enrichment of that freedom under the Commonwealth. His confirmation and refutation verify that Scripture supports the regicides: Britain is actualizing the will of God. False prophets and backsliders, enemies of Reformation bent on misleading the nation, are the targets of his satiric slashes. England in 1649, he believes, has bravely rid itself of corrupt kingship and is fully capable of further enlightened response to the "Supreme Magistracy."

As it was in *The Tenure*, Milton's rhetoric of vehemence in *Prelatical Episcopacy* and *Tetrachordon* is aimed not at the British people, but at decadent institutions and self-seeking leaders. His denunciation of episcopacy has as its object popish ceremonies and outmoded traditions which sit, Juno-like, to block the birth of Reformation, and not the national character. Milton's repeated appeals to Scripture in *Prelatical Episcopacy* are emphatic in their assertion that God champions the Puritan cause. The very act of translating abstract, academic issues into easily understood terms in both *Prelatical Episcopacy* and *Tetrachordon* bespeaks Milton's faith in the ability of the citizenry to grasp the essence of each controversy. Even the harsh indictments in the books of the *History of Britain* written in the 1640's work principally by analogy: the barrier of time shields the seventeenth century from the full force of Milton's rhetoric. Moreover, Milton does not intend to scorn the English public in the *History*, but to alert them, their leaders, and their institutions to the pitfalls on the path to Reformation. He is confident that all will respond.

Yet the *History* also anticipates the Miltonic vision of liberty which was to predominate in the 1650's, a vision growing progressively sharper in its focus; for the *History* records the "unsound" deeds of entire nations, not merely of individuals, and its memorable Digression casts a foreboding shadow on the present. That vision is discordant, fragmented, less immediate, and, as a consequence, more personal in its emphasis than was the utopian perspective of the 1640's. In the 1650's Milton's rhetoric of excoriation is broader in scope than it was earlier, and the English people themselves, not popish practices or monarchial abuses, are likely to be its subjects. Milton has been forced to acknowledge that the nation is more than willing to barter its priceless liberty for the most dubious of gains, that the Commonwealth and its Reformed leaders are little better than the king and prelates they displaced. The tracts of the 1650's we have examined lack the vivid, half-poetic dramatizations of Reformation realized which had marked the 1640's. Instead, Milton's voice is often Jeremiac in its bitter admission that the prophet must minister to an unheeding rabble. In the 1650's, rather than celebrating the potential for liberty and the actual forward steps taken by the nation, Milton is moved, most obviously in *The Readie Way*, to denounce his people for the magnitude of their failures. His despair over the attainment of the New Jerusalem on earth flows into the ironic stances so evident in the 1650's. Milton's weariness over narrating the lot of errant mankind in the *History of Britain* eventually overwhelmed him. He was to see the disheartening postlapsarian yearning for slavery recur in 1659-1660. Again, he ends his remarks on an ironic, resigned note.

The tracts of 1659-1660, and the fact that Milton delayed publication of his *History* until 1670, point to a profound change in his concept of the audience for whom he wrote and in the direction of his rhetoric itself. Joan Webber has theorized that Milton, like other Puritan authors, conceived of each of his tracts as a "model for conversion," as an "incentive for revolutionary action," or as a "record of truth for future generations."[126] I would suggest that Milton intended the documents published in the 1640's primarily as incentives for "revolutionary action," while those of the 1650's are justified by their achievement of the other two ends. Milton became convinced as the 1650's wore on that his rhetoric was virtually powerless to affect the onrushing course of public events, that his prophetic vision was not destined to issue in a Reformed nation. This is not to say that Milton forsakes his attempt to define idealized patterns of behavior which, if imitated, would speed the attainment of Reformation. In Book V of the *History* he offers in Alfred a paradigm of regenerate political leadership, and in *Hirelings* and *The Readie Way* plans for a non-mercenary clergy and a just Parliament, respectively. He could, in conscience, do no less. Yet it is equally true that the inspiring eulogies of Reformed leaders and institutions prevalent in the 1640's do not occur in the writings of the 1650's we have examined. Increasingly, as he does in *The Readie Way* and *Hirelings*, Milton must distance himself personally from the events he describes, for they no longer merit celebration. Neither the kingship he laments in *The Readie Way* nor the vicious circle of human corruption he uncovers in the *History* is personally palatable. Public and personal truth have polarized.

Milton's hopes in the 1650's do not rest with institutions or with politicians, for he had seen both come to naught, but rather with the "fit audience though few" of regenerate readers. Those readers, he assumes, will be receptive to the dualistic thrust of the sermons of 1659-1660 and the *History of Britain*, each of which is a form of metaphoric discourse whose full implications are perceivable by the regenerate reader alone. Although all of these pamphlets may be read for their public relevance to Reformation, the spiritually sensitive reader will also detect in them the unfolding of regenerate response to experience. In each work the narrative presence replaces the public articulation of Milton's dream of Reformation as the thematic center. Although the narrator must denounce the corrupt world around him, his very denunciation is an elevating example of Christian liberty at work. In effect, readers who have not already forfeited their freedom will discover in the tracts of 1659-1660 and the *History* "models of conversion" and sources of spiritual enrichment on a personal level. Prompted by the example of the Miltonic persona, they may set out to fortify the inner kingdom against the onslaughts of unregeneracy.

The divergence of public truth and personal witness in the works of the 1650's also accounts for a profound change in the aesthetic impulses behind Milton's rhetoric. Their persuasive, homiletic objectives justified the tracts published in the 1640's. In his last major pamphlet, *The Readie Way*, Milton advances quite another rationale, one implied in *Civil Power* and *Hirelings*, and perhaps reenforced by the late publication date of his *History*. Although circumstances had forced Milton to conclude that the public impact of his rhetoric was severely limited, that at best its inner meaning might be deciphered and applied by the regenerate few, he ultimately found the message of liberty worth proclaiming for its own sake. Milton's final important treatises are justified by the motive which inspired his poetry, one which transcends the utilitarian bounds of propagandistic polemic. With his voice of witness he records for posterity eternal Christian truths which are ends in themselves and valid whether they be embodied in a Holy Community or kept alive by the lonely witness of a solitary individual.

Notes to Chapter I

1. *A Second Defence*, in *Complete Prose Works of John Milton*, ed. Don M. Wolfe et al. (New Haven: Yale Univ. Press, 1966), IV, 624. I have used the Yale Edition throughout this study, except in Chapter V, where I use the Columbia Edition for treatises that have not yet appeared in the Yale *Prose Works*; subsequent references will be to volume and page.

2. *Milton and the Puritan Dilemma, 1641-1660* (Toronto: Univ. of Toronto Press, 1942), pp. xvii-xviii.

3. A.S.P. Woodhouse, "Milton, Puritanism, and Liberty," *UTQ*, 4 (1935), 498. I concur with Woodhouse's premise that Milton emphasized the ethical character of Christian freedom (p. 498).

4. *The Return of Eden: Five Essays on Milton's Epics* (Toronto: Univ. of Toronto Press, 1965), p. 94.

5. *On Christian Doctrine*, trans. D. W. Robertson, Jr. (Indianapolis: Liberal Arts Press, 1958), Bk. IV, Chs. II, XI.

6. *Brutus and Orator*, trans. G. L. Hendrickson and H. M. Hubbell, Loeb Classical Library (Cambridge, Mass.: Harvard Univ. Press, 1952), xxi. 71-72. Subsequent references will be to the Loeb Edition.

7. *Rhetorica*, trans. W. Rhys Roberts, in *The Works of Aristotle Translated into English*, gen. ed. W. D. Ross (Oxford: Clarendon Press, 1924), 11, Bk. I, Ch. III. Subsequent references to the works of Aristotle will be to volume, book, and section in the Oxford Edition.

8. Ibid., Bk. I, Ch. II, 1356a.

9. *De Partitione Oratoria*, trans. Horace Rackham, Loeb Classical Library (Cambridge, Mass.: Harvard Univ. Press, 1948), vi. 20. Subsequent references will be to the Loeb Edition.

10. *Institutio Oratoria*, trans. H. E. Butler, Loeb Classical Library (New York: Putnam, 1922), Vol. IV, Bk. XII, x. 62. See also Vol. III, Bk. IX, 11. 26-40. Subsequent references will be to the Loeb Edition.

11. *Orator*, xxv. 84 - xxv. 86.

12. *Rhetorica Ad Herennium*, trans. Harry Caplan, Loeb Classical Library (Cambridge, Mass.: Harvard Univ. Press, 1954), Bk. IV, x. 14. The authorship of the *Ad Herennium* remains uncertain. Used by Cicero and once attributed to him, the treatise is now thought to have been composed by Cornificius.

13. *Orator*, xxvi. 87 - xxvi. 90.

14. *Orator*, xxvi. 91 - xxviii. 97. For useful discussions of classical and Renaissance stylistic theory, see G. L. Hendrickson, "The Peripatetic Mean of Style and the Three Stylistic Characters," *AJP*, 25 (1904), 125-46, and "The Origin and Meaning of the Ancient Characters of Style," *AJP*, 26 (1905), 249-90; Walter F. Staton, "The Characters of Style in Elizabethan Prose," *JEGP*, 57 (1958), 197-207.

15. See Herbert J. C. Grierson, *Milton and Wordsworth, Poets and Prophets: A Study of Their Reactions to Political Events* (New York: MacMillan, 1937), Ch. II; Wittreich, "The Crown of Eloquence," pp. 9-11.

16. *The Confessions,* in *The Library of Christian Classics,* trans. Albert C. Outler (Philadelphia: Westminster Press, 1955), VII, Bk. X.

17. For a concise summary of the literal-to-symbolic thrust of Augustine's rhetoric, see Joseph A. Mazzeo, "St. Augustine's Rhetoric of Silence: Truth vs. Eloquence and Things vs. Signs," in *Renaissance and Seventeenth-Century Studies* (New York: Columbia Univ. Press, 1964), pp. 1-28.

18. Ronald H. Nash, *The Light of the Mind: St. Augustine's Theory of Knowledge* (Lexington: Univ. Press of Kentucky, 1968), pp. 4-9. As Nash argues, Augustine's theories of epistemology show thorough Platonic overtones, overtones which are, in turn, reflected in Milton. The relationship of Plato's theory of knowledge to Milton's aesthetic has recently been reasserted by Michael Lieb, "Milton and the Metaphysics of Form," *SP,* 71 (1974), 206-24.

19. Irene Samuel, *Plato and Milton* (Ithaca: Cornell Univ. Press, 1947), p. 139.

20. Nash, pp. 34-35.

21. John Donne uses an analogous rhetorical strategy in his sermons. His debt to Augustinian homiletic is shown by Dennis Quinn in "Donne's Christian Eloquence," *ELH,* 27 (1960), 276-97, and by Robert L. Hickey in two articles: "Donne's Art of Memory," *Tennessee Studies in Literature,* 3 (1958), 29-36, and "Donne's Art of Preaching," *Tennessee Studies in Literature,* 1 (1956), 65-74. See also William Haller, *The Rise of Puritanism* (New York: Harper and Row, 1957), Ch. II. Haller notes that the Puritan sermon "commonly labored to escape from abstract to imagistic methods of presenting doctrine" (p. 143).

22. See Augustine, *The Teacher,* in *The Library of Christian Classics,* trans. John H. S. Burleigh (Philadelphia: Westminster Press, 1953), VI, Ch. XII.

23. Hickey, "Donne's Art of Memory," pp. 33-34.

24. *The Eloquent "I": Style and Self in Seventeenth-Century Prose* (Madison: Univ. of Wisconsin Press, 1968), p. 207.

25. Frye, *The Return of Eden,* p. 110.

26. Louis Martz, *The Paradise Within: Studies in Vaughan, Traherne, and Milton* (New Haven: Yale Univ. Press, 1964), p. 131.

27. I have employed the following stylistic terminology; the categories I have established are based upon syntax, the lowest common denominator among Milton's various styles. Milton's periodic style has been defined effectively by K. G. Hamilton ("The Structure of Milton's Prose," in *Language and Style in Milton,* ed. Emma and Shawcross [New York: Ungar, 1967], pp. 304-32). Hamilton claims that in a periodic sentence "the main idea remains suspended while additions and qualifications are introduced" (p. 308), and that periodic sentences tend to be lengthy and given to hypotactic rather than paratactic linkage (p. 307). Milton's low, middle, and high oratorical styles are overwhelmingly periodic; periodic structures also occur often in the *History of Britain* and in the disputative pamphlets discussed in Chapter Four. More prevalent than periodicity in the seventeenth century was the curt- or loose-Senecan mode, as described by Morris Croll ("The Ba-

roque Style in Prose," in *Style, Rhetoric, and Rhythm: Essays by Morris W. Croll,* ed. J. Max. Patrick et al. [Princeton, N. J.: Princeton Univ. Press, 1966], pp. 207-33). In the curt-Senecan style we find short, elliptical sentence members, a complete absence of connectives, and a studied asymmetry of parts. The loose style, on the other hand, accumulates clauses and phrases serially and prefers coordinate linkage and absolute constructions. Theoretically, the loose style ought to record the "movements of a mind discovering truth as it goes." Curt- and loose-Senecan sentences appear in Milton's prose with much less frequency than do periodic ones, their greatest concentration being in the *History of Britain.* A third syntactical paradigm, prevalent in the last quarter of the seventeenth century, is perhaps derived from Senecanism. I refer to the plain, direct prose favored by many Restoration writers, prose which is syntactically linear instead of periodic. Yet, the typical plain sentence, unlike the typical Senecan sentence, is generally structured in the manner of subject-verb-object. I shall examine Milton's use of this pattern in Chapter Five.

28. "Milton and the Marprelate Tradition," *MiltonS,* 8 (1975), 103-21.

29. Fletcher, *The Intellectual Development of John Milton,* 2 vols. (Urbana: Univ. of Illinois Press, 1956-1961); Clark, *John Milton at St. Paul's School* (New York: Columbia Univ. Press, 1948).

30. See Wittreich, "The Crown of Eloquence"; Wilbur Elwyn Gilman, *Milton's Rhetoric: Studies in His Defense of Liberty,* 2nd ed. (1939; rpt. New York: Phaeton Press, 1970); Keith W. Stavely, *The Politics of Milton's Prose Style* (New Haven: Yale Univ. Press, 1975). Stavely's book reached me after this manuscript was completed. He has at least succeeded in establishing a thesis which allows him to deal with the entire prose period, namely that one may evaluate Milton's political theories in light of his syntactical patterns.

Notes to Chapter II

31. I have selected these tracts because they are the most sophisticated, polished examples of Milton's oratorical mode. The stylistic strategies of *Areopagitica* are anticipated in *Of Reformation* (1641), and those of *The Tenure* in *Doctrine and Discipline of Divorce* (1644). For a discussion of oratorical techniques in *Of Reformation* and *Doctrine and Discipline,* see my doctoral dissertation, "The Varieties of Style in Milton's Prose," Notre Dame 1971, Ch. II. Of course, the *Prolusions* allowed Milton to rehearse the stylistic tactics evident in all of the orations of the 1640's. I have not reviewed the rhetoric of Milton's academic orations because of the attention paid to the subject by others. See Wittreich, "The Crown of Eloquence"; Thomas R. Hartmann, "Milton's *Prolusions*: A Study," Diss. N.Y.U. 1962; Dan Stead Collins, "Rhetoric and Logic in Milton's English Poems," Diss. North Carolina 1960, Ch. II.

32. *Ethica Nichomachea,* Vol. IX, Bk. III, Chs. X-XI.

33. *Institutio Oratoria,* Vol. II, Bk. IV, 1. 60-61.

94

34. Gilman, *Milton's Rhetoric*, p. 12. See pp. 9-44 for a complete listing of Milton's varieties of rhetorical proof.

35. II, 496, n. 37.

36. Ibid., n. 38.

37. Both Gilman (p. 15) and Ernest Sirluck (II, 166-67) agree that the position and length of the final argument denote its importance, although neither relates Milton's positioning of the argument to his thematic intentions.

38. II, 171. In fact, the "national digression" is harmonized with the rest of the oration through its style, tone, and persona.

39. *Institutio Oratoria*, Vol. II, Bk. IV, 1. 28-29; *De Partitione Oratoria*, xiv. 52 - xvii. 60.

40. II, 564, n. 278.

41. Charles S. Baldwin, *Medieval Rhetoric and Poetic*, 2nd ed. (1928; rpt. New York: Peter Smith, 1959), p. 67.

42. Mazzeo, "St. Augustine's Rhetoric of Silence," pp. 1-11.

43. For an analysis of the genre and structure of the oration, see John T. Shawcross, ed., *The Tenure of Kings and Magistrates*, in *The Prose of John Milton*, gen. ed. J. Max Patrick (New York: Anchor Books, 1967), p. 341. Milton's arguments have been categorized by Gilman, *Milton's Rhetoric*, pp. 99-110. The logical thrust of Milton's style is examined by M. Y. Hughes, III, 128-35. My discussion touches on only the first (1649) edition. Although the second (1650) edition appends a list of citations from Presbyterian authorities, it does not alter substantially the argument of the first.

44. Jer. 48: 10 (III, 191, n. 4).

45. Prov. 12: 10 (III, 193, n. 15).

46. I Sam. 15: 33 (III, 193, n. 16).

47. I Sam. 14: 1-45 (III, 194, n. 17).

48. These three Scriptural figures (Num. 16: 12-35) were agents of political dissension, rebels against the government of Moses and Aaron (III, 56-58).

49. III, 108.

50. Jgs. 3: 14-15 (III, 213, n. 85).

51. II Kgs. 9: 7-25 (III, 215, n. 91).

52. For a general explication of Milton's use of historical analogy in *The Tenure*, see Noreen L. Hayes, "Some Implications of Milton's Philosophy of History," Diss. Northwestern 1969, pp. 140-56. Her emphasis falls upon historiography rather than rhetoric.

53. For example, III, 222: "if the Church in all ages . . . . to the cutting off without exemption him that capitally offends."

Notes to Chapter III

54. See Irene Samuel, "Milton and the Ancients on the Writing of History," *MS*, 2 (1970), 133-40. Professor Samuel is perhaps the strongest proponent of the view that facts alone were Milton's concern when he

wrote the *History*. Her study explores the implications of Milton's 1657 letter to Henry de Brass, virtually ignoring, unfortunately, the substantial body of didactic comments in the tract.

55. For summaries of the humanist philosophy of history, see Lily B. Campbell, *Shakespeare's "Histories": Mirrors of Elizabethan Policy* (San Marino, Calif.: The Huntington Library, 1947), Chs. I-III; Felix Gilbert, *Machiavelli and Guicciardini: Politics and History in Sixteenth-Century Florence* (Princeton, N. J.: Princeton Univ. Press, 1965), pp. 203-35. See also C. A. Patrides, *Milton and the Christian Tradition* (Oxford: Clarendon Press, 1966), Ch. VIII.

56. "Milton as Historian," in Fogle and H. R. Trevor-Roper, *Milton and Clarendon* (Los Angeles: Clark Library, 1965), p. 4; my italics.

57. "John Milton's *History of Britain*: Its Place in English Historiography," *University of Mississippi Studies in English*, 6 (1965), 68-69.

58. Peter Gay, *A Loss of Mastery: Puritan Historians in Colonial America* (Berkeley: Univ. of Calif. Press, 1966), p. 17.

59. G. L. Keyes, *Christian Faith and the Interpretation of History: A Study of St. Augustine's Philosophy of History* (Lincoln: Univ. of Nebraska Press, 1966), p. 190. I am especially indebted to Ch. VI of Keyes' study.

60. Ibid.

61. "Milton as Historian," p. 17.

62. V, 165, n. 76. Fogle confesses to uncertainty about the precise meaning of "trivial." I think it fair to infer, however, Milton's skepticism about the validity of Nennius' judgments in this particular context.

63. Ibid., n. 75.

64. Ibid., n. 77.

65. *Tacitus* (Oxford: Clarendon Press, 1958), I, 197.

66. Ibid.

67. *Ben Jonson's Poems: A Study of the Plain Style* (Stanford, Calif.: Stanford Univ. Press, 1962), p. 28.

68. *Orator*, xi. 37 - xii. 38.

69. Augustine argued, of course, that the Christian historian possessed prophetic spiritual insight into the mass of historical data he dealt with. See R. A. Markus, *Saeculum: History and Society in the Theology of St. Augustine* (Cambridge: The University Press, 1970), pp. 195-96.

70. J. A. Bryant, Jr., "The Evolution of Milton's Conception of History," Diss. Yale 1948, p. 226.

71. *Essays Historical and Literary* (Oxford: Clarendon Press, 1938), p. 101.

72. The reason for the Digression's omission when the *History* was published in 1670 is, I think, plain enough. As an incitement to continue Reformation of church and state, the document had lost its effectiveness. This is, of course, the view advanced by Masson and seconded by Firth. See Fogle's discussion (V, 409-14).

73. V, 317, n. 97.

74. V, 282, n. 35.

75. The matter of dates is far from certain, but there is little doubt that Books V and VI, and perhaps part of IV were composed after 1652 (V, xli-xliii).

76. "Milton as Historian," p. 16.

77. V, 394, n. 99.

Notes to Chapter IV

78. J. Max Patrick and Arthur M. Axelrad, eds., "The Divorce Tracts," in *The Prose of John Milton,* gen. ed. Patrick, p. 213.

79. Patrick and Axelrad have also noted (p. 210) the scholarly nature of these tracts. In none of his other polemic works is Milton's learning so much in evidence.

80. William T. Costello, S. J., *The Scholastic Curriculum at Early Seventeenth-Century Cambridge* (Cambridge, Mass.: Harvard Univ. Press, 1958), p. 11.

81. Fletcher, *The Intellectual Development of John Milton,* II, 238.

82. Richard McKeon, "Rhetoric in the Middle Ages," *Speculum,* 17 (1942), 11.

83. These manuals, written and reprinted during the sixteenth century, circulated widely during the seventeenth. John Seton's *Dialectica* (1545), a scholastic logic popular at Cambridge, reiterates the advice of Fraunce and Wilson. See Fletcher, pp. 247ff., for a discussion of the textbooks of logic in use at Cambridge.

84. *The Rule of Reason; Conteining the Art of Logike* (London, 1567), fol. 63v. Wilson is hereafter cited in the text. The passage is also quoted by Sister Miriam Joseph, *Shakespeare's Use of the Arts of Language* (New York: Columbia Univ. Press, 1947), p. 376. For a compact analysis of the art of disputation in the Renaissance, see Miriam Joseph, pp. 375-85. My subsequent argument is indebted to her research.

85. Aristotle's primary commentary on artificial proof occurs in the *Rhetoric,* Vol. 11, Bk. I, Ch. XV.

86. *The Lawiers Logike . . .* (1588; facsimile rpt. Yorkshire: Scolar Press, 1969), fol. 102v. The manual first appeared in 1551. I borrow, with some modifications, Miriam Joseph's outline arrangement (pp. 377-80) of Fraunce's precepts.

87. The tropes above are cited in Miriam Joseph, p. 383.

88. Hartmann, "Milton's *Prolusions*: A Study," pp. 7, 9-11.

89. I, 259, n. 6.

90. See also I, 619. J. Max Patrick has called attention to Milton's "brilliant debating" in *Prelatical Episcopacy,* and theorized that Milton was attempting to appeal to a "wider public than the erudite theologians and scholars to whom Ussher's pamphlet would have appealed." I concur with this thesis; my discussion of *Prelatical Episcopacy* will illustrate the rhetorical character of Milton's appeal.

91. *Jeremy Taylor and the Great Rebellion: A Study of His Mind and Temper in Controversy* (Ann Arbor: Univ. of Michigan Press, 1970), pp. 13ff.

92. Ibid., p. 13.

93. Ibid., p. 19.

94. Hall's *Episcopacie* was published in February of 1640 (I, 653), while both Ussher's *Judgement* and Almoni's *Discourse* appeared in May, 1641 (I, 619). A publication date of June or July, 1641, has been assigned to *Prelatical Episcopacy* (I, 619).

95. Miriam Joseph, p. 382.

96. See I, 636, n. 40. As J. Max Patrick observes, the authorship of this passage is disputed. Understandably, Milton felt no obligation to distinguish among doctrines actually formulated by Ignatius and those merely attributed to him.

97. The transition from logical to evocative argument begins on I, 639-40, as Milton starts to ridicule the numerous errors which mar the testimony of the "authorities" venerated by episcopacy. Appeals to logic and authority do appear, on occasion, in the remainder of the tract, but Milton's rhetorical emphasis has clearly shifted to evocative ploys.

98. This "narration" is not supported by scholarly citation, nor is it connected logically to the arguments which enclose it. Digression is, of course, one of the weapons of dispute sanctioned by Wilson.

99. Williams' explanatory notes on *Tetrachordon* in the Yale Edition identify the commentaries Milton favors. There are in these tracts incidental analogues to Milton's exegetical procedures, but the specifics of his rhetorical strategy are, to my knowledge, without parallel.

100. The argument from Deut. is structured as follows: affirmation and refutation (II, 614-27); polemic (II, 627-35). Although appeals to logic can be found in the polemical sections of the argument, the gradual shift from logic to evocation is clearly evident.

Notes to Chapter V

101. Milton's "brevitie" has not passed unnoticed. See Kenneth Muir, *John Milton* (London: Longmans, Green and Company, 1955), p. 99; Barbara Lewalski, ed., *A Treatise of Civil Power in Ecclesiastical Causes,* in *The Prose of John Milton*, gen. ed. Patrick, p. 443. Muir observes that the prose of Milton's "last period" is as "plain and direct as that demanded by the anti-imaginative members of the Royal Society," and Mrs. Lewalski reaches virtually the same conclusion concerning *Civil Power*. For a non-historical approach to the rhetoric of the tract, see Harry Smallenburg, "Government of the Spirit: Style, Structure and Theme in *Treatise of Civil Power*," in *Achievements of the Left Hand*, pp. 219-38. Syntactical in emphasis, Smallenburg's study examines the exotic effects he theorizes Milton's style will have on his readers. For the most part, I find Smallenburg's thesis unconvincing, particularly his assertion (p. 233) that the pamphlet's argu-

ment fails to "conform to any strictly laid out organizational plan." I shall argue that precisely the opposite is true. In this Chapter, all references are to the Columbia Edition unless they are preceded by *CP* (Yale *Complete Prose*).

102. Jones, "Science and English Prose Style in the Third Quarter of the Seventeenth Century," *PMLA,* 45 (1930), 977-1009.

103. *The Rise of Modern Prose Style* (Cambridge, Mass.: MIT Press, 1968).

104. Miller, *The New England Mind: The Seventeenth Century* (Boston: Beacon Press, 1961), Chs. V, XII; Fisch, "The Puritans and the Reform of Prose Style," *ELH,* 19 (1952), 229-48.

105. *Preaching in England in the Late Fifteenth and Sixteenth Centuries* (Oxford: Basil Blackwell, 1964), Ch. III.

106. *History of the Royal Society,* ed. Jackson Cope and H. W. Jones (St. Louis: Washington Univ. Press, 1958), p. 113.

107. Adolph, *The Rise of Modern Prose Style,* p. 249.

108. Ibid., p. 248.

109. Ibid., p. 247.

110. *Ecclesiastes,* pp. 5-20. Wilkins was equally well known for his stylistic edicts. In *Ecclesiastes* he urged that the language of preaching "must be plain and naturall, not being darkned with the affectation of Scholastical harshness, or Rhetorical flourishes . . . . When the notion it self is good, the best way to set it off, is in the most obvious plain expression" (p. 72). Similar sentiments dot his *Discourse Concerning the Gift of Prayer* (1653). See also *Three Restoration Divines: Barrow, South, Tillotson,* ed. Iréne Simon, Bibliothèque de la Faculté de Philosophie et Lettres de l'Université de Liège, Fascicule 181 (Paris, 1967), I, 41-46.

111. Simon's analyses of Barrow, South, and Tillotson are persuasive proof of this point.

112. Barker, *Milton and the Puritan Dilemma,* pp. 272-73.

113. See, for example, VI, 19: "No protestant therfore . . . ought . . . to be forc'd or molested for religion."

114. Rhetorical figures in the passage include the following: alliteration; *polysyndeton;* antithesis and *isocolon*: "suffering . . . Flesh . . . triumphing . . . Spirit." The "ascendant parallel metaphor" (I, 519), which associates Christ's suffering and death with the trials of his Church, unifies the thought pattern of the sentence by fusing body and spirit, past and present, the literal and the symbolic.

115. Adolph argues (p. 248) that the use of adjectives for logical instead of rhetorical purposes is characteristic of the Restoration "Prose of Utility."

116. The closest analogue in the Milton canon to the plain style of *Civil Power, Hirelings,* and *The Readie Way* is the historical narrative style in the *History of Britain.* In both styles we find short sentence members usually linked by coordinating conjunctions, a diminished role for an authorial persona, and an absence of figurative display. Yet there are also marked differences. The tracts of 1659-1660 indicate

a thorough Miltonic participation in the reductive aesthetic summed up by Sprat. That participation is evident in each tract's structure and argumentative strategy as well as in its style. Moreover, while sentence members in the historical style are verb-centered, those in the plain style are noun-centered. The subject-verb-object paradigm predominant in 1659-1660 occurs rarely in the *History*.

117. Milton examines in *Hirelings*: "what recompence God hath ordaind should be given to ministers of the church . . . next by whom; and lastly, in what manner" (VI, 50). The cumulative effect of these arguments is to urge the removal of hirelings.

118. See especially VI, 73: Gal. 6: 6; I Cor. 9: 11; I Tim. 5: 17.

119. Milton's repeated allusions to the gentilish practice of kingship forbidden by Christ (e.g., VI, 124, 130-31, 136-37) define gentilism metaphorically as a form of antichristian heathenism.

120. Barbara Lewalski observes that the second edition appeared after April 20, 1660, less than two weeks before the return of Charles from France (*The Prose of John Milton*, gen. ed. Patrick, p. 522). The fact that the second edition records Milton's final and most emphatic reaction toward imminent chaos renders its rhetorical significance greater than that of the first edition.

121. Cf. Stavely, *The Politics of Milton's Prose Style*, pp. 98-111. Concentrating upon Milton's syntax, Stavely locates a duality in the pamphlet's rhetoric. Although our arguments are analogous at times, his general approach to the dualism and his conclusions about it differ substantially from my own.

122. The historical context of the Treaty is explored by Samuel R. Gardiner, *History of the Great Civil War, 1642-1649*, 2nd ed. (1898; rpt. New York: AMS Press, 1965), IV, Ch. LXVI.

Notes to Chapter VI

123. See Barker, *Milton and the Puritan Dilemma*, Chs. VIII-XV; Don M. Wolfe, *Milton in the Puritan Revolution* (London: Nelson, 1941), Chs. XIII-XIV; William Haller, *Liberty and Reformation in the Puritan Revolution* (New York: Columbia Univ. Press, 1955), Ch. X.

124. Haller, p. 358.

125. Ibid., p. 354.

126. Webber, *The Eloquent "I,"* p. 251.